P9-CJN-705

3 1404 00755 7074

THE COMMONWEALTH AND INTE...

Joint Chairmen of the Honorary Edit...

SIR ROBERT ROBINSON, O.M., F.R.S., LONDON

DEAN ATHELSTAN SPILHAUS, MINNESOTA

LATIN-AMERICAN DIVISION

General Editor: G. BROTHERSTON

CÉSAR VALLEJO

AN A...OLOGY OF HIS POETRY

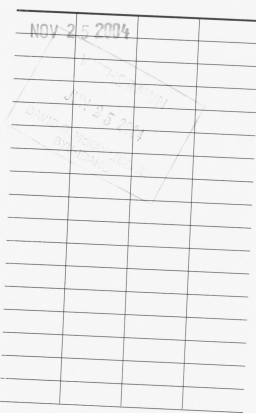

DATE DUE

CÉSAR VALLEJO

AN ANTHOLOGY OF HIS POETRY

With an Introduction and Notes by

JAMES HIGGINS

Lecturer in Latin-American Literature,
The University of Liverpool

PERGAMON PRESS

Oxford · New York · Toronto · Sydney · Braunschweig

Pergamon Press Ltd., Headington Hill Hall, Oxford

Pergamon Press Inc., Maxwell House, Fairview Park, Elmsford,
New York 10523

Pergamon of Canada Ltd., 207 Queen's Quay West, Toronto 1

Pergamon Press (Aust.) Pty. Ltd., 19a Boundary Street,
Rushcutters Bay, N.S.W. 2011, Australia

Vieweg & Sohn GmbH, Burgplatz 1, Braunschweig

First edition 1970

Library of Congress Catalog Card No. 75–110410

Printed in Great Britain by A. Wheaton & Co., Exeter

CONTENTS

FOREWORD

César Vallejo is one of the great poets of the Spanish language. He is also perhaps the most difficult, with the possible exception of Góngora. The difficulty of his work has created a special problem in the preparation of this edition, for limitations of space make it impossible to explain every obscurity and, in any case, many explanations could only be tentative. I have compromised by keeping the notes to a minimum and making the Introduction longer than originally intended. In the Introduction I have avoided generalizing as far as possible and referred to the poems included in the anthology, and I have attempted to give a brief interpretation of each poem in the hope that this will clarify the general sense and enable the reader to go on to a deeper study.

The texts of the poems are based on the first editions of Vallejo's poetry and on the edition of his *Obra poética completa*, which was prepared under the direction of Georgette de Vallejo, the poet's widow. I am indebted to Señora de Vallejo for biographical information.

INTRODUCTION

I

CÉSAR VALLEJO (1892–1938)

César Abraham Vallejo was born in March 1892 (probably the 16th) in the small town of Santiago de Chuco in northern Peru. His ancestry—his two grandfathers were Spanish, his grandmothers Indian—made him a *cholo*, or *mestizo*. He was also a *serrano*, for Santiago is situated at a height of 10,500 feet in a valley in the *sierra*. It has been claimed, not very convincingly, that these factors of heredity and environment shaped his poetry, that his work expresses the pessimism, defeatism, resignation and sense of abandonment of the Indian and the desolation of the bleak, inhospitable Andean region. Much more important is the family atmosphere in which Vallejo grew up. Despite hardships—his family belonged to the rural middle class and, without being really poor, was never comfortably off—he enjoyed a contented and integrated childhood. César was the youngest of eleven children and the family was united by strong bonds of affection. Throughout his life he identified happiness with the home and the family, which was always one of his great ideals, and he always retained a particular affection and reverence for his mother as the incarnation of love and the directing force behind the family. He was also brought up in an atmosphere of religious piety. Both of his grandfathers had been priests and they had bequeathed to the family a rich collection of religious books. Though Vallejo was to move away from religion, this Christian formation determined many of his attitudes, notably his ideal of brotherly love, and his reading of the Bible furnished him with much of his imagery.

1

Having received his primary education in Santiago and his secondary schooling in the nearby town of Huamachuco, Vallejo spent two years at home, apparently undecided as to what to do with his life. In 1911 he went to Lima to study medicine but soon abandoned the course. He then took a job as tutor of the children of a *hacendado* on an estate near Huánuco. The following year he worked as assistant cashier on a sugar plantation, the *Hacienda Roma*. There his eyes were opened to social injustice and to the oppression and exploitation of the workers, and the memory of what he saw was lasting.

In the years 1913–17 Vallejo studied *Letras* and Law at the *Universidad de la Libertad* in Trujillo (capital of the department of which Santiago is a province), financing his studies by working as a schoolteacher. He seems to have taken a particular interest in the courses on Spanish Literature and was an avid reader of Spanish classical writers. In 1915 he graduated as *Bachiller en Letras*, presenting a thesis entitled *El romanticismo en la poesía castellana*.

Vallejo apparently had had literary aspirations for some time and it was in Trujillo that he began writing seriously. However, the conservative and traditionally minded Trujillo, a city that had scarcely changed since colonial times, was hardly an encouraging environment for an aspiring young poet. Moreover, Vallejo himself had grown up in a cultural desert and was remarkably behind the times in his reading, for his knowledge of modern literature did not extend beyond post-Romanticism and such writers as Manuel Acuña and Salvador Díaz Mirón.

The end of 1915 marked a turning-point in Vallejo's life, for he entered into contact with a group of progressive young writers and intellectuals. Leaders of the group were the artist, José Eulogio Garrido, editor of *La Industria*, and the essayist and philosopher, Antenor Orrego, editor of *La Reforma*. The group also included the poets Alcides Spelucín, Francisco Sandoval and Oscar Imaña, the painter Macedonio de la Torre, and the politician Víctor Raúl Haya de la Torre. Orrego in particular encouraged and advised the young poet. Through his contact with the group Vallejo extended his reading to embrace Spanish American Modernists such as Julio Herrera y Reissig, Rubén Darío, José Santos Chocano, and Amado Nervo; the American Walt Whitman; a number of French symbolists such as Samain, Jammes, Maeterlinck, Verlaine, Rimbaud. A number of Vallejo's poems were published in *La Industria* and *La Reforma* in the years 1916–18.

In Trujillo Vallejo had a number of amorous adventures. The most serious was his affair with Zoila Rosa Cuadra in 1917. This affair broke up after a series of quarrels and it has been said that this precipitated Vallejo's departure for Lima in the last days of 1917. In fact this move was inevitable. Trujillo was narrow and backward and Vallejo and his fellow intellectuals were treated with derision and hostility. A more propitious environment was needed if Vallejo was to develop his genius: to fulfil himself as a poet he had to move to the capital, as later he was to move to Europe.

The early days of 1918 saw Vallejo in Lima with few friends and little money. However, he was not unknown in the capital, for some of his poems had appeared in reviews. He was well received by such prominent writers as Abraham Valdelomar, Manuel González Prada and José María Eguren, and he was soon moving in the capital's literary circles. He obtained a post in a primary school and continued his studies in the University of San Marcos. In August he suffered a great personal loss, the death of his mother. Meanwhile he had been preparing *Los heraldos negros* for publication but the volume did not appear till July 1919. It had a mixed reception.

In September 1918, on the death of the director, Vallejo and two colleagues took over the school with the poet as director. For a time it prospered but by the early months of 1919 it had run into economic difficulties and there was dissension between Vallejo and his partners. Since the middle of 1918 Vallejo had been having a love-affair with a certain Otilia,[1] the sister-in-law of

[1] Further details of this affair are given by Juan Espejo Asturrizaga, *César Vallejo. Itinerario del hombre*, Lima, 1965, pp. 68–76. Espejo conceals Otilia's surname.

one of his partners. Vallejo seems to have been a difficult, if ardent, lover and the affair was punctuated by quarrels. After a while he found himself at odds with Otilia's family—in particular, her brother-in-law, who was head of the household—who wished to press him into marriage. By the middle of 1919 the situation had become impossible and Vallejo abandoned the school and broke with Otilia.

In July 1920 Vallejo returned to his home in Santiago for the festivities in honour of the town's patron saint. In the course of the festivities local enmities, fanned by drunkenness, flared up into a riot in which the town's most important business house was burned and sacked. An innocent bystander, Vallejo found himself involved because of his family connections. Charges were placed against him and nineteen others and for some two and a half months he took refuge in Antenor Orrego's country cottage just outside Trujillo. He was eventually arrested in November and spent 112 days in prison in Trujillo before being released in February of the following year, the charges unproved.

In March 1921 Vallejo returned to Lima where he again took up a teaching post. For some time he had been preparing a second book of verse and he had also been writing prose. In 1922 he won a prize for his short story *Más allá de la vida y la muerte*, and he published *Trilce*. New and revolutionary in its poetic expression, *Trilce* met with a cold reception. In the following year Vallejo published *Escalas melografiadas*, a collection of short stories, and *Fabla salvaje*, a short novel. The prose is mediocre but throws considerable light on the poetry.

In 1923 Vallejo set sail for Europe, a trip he had been planning for some time. He arrived in Paris in July with little money and few connections and ignorant of the language. During the next two years he suffered great hardship: he moved from one cheap hotel to another and at times had nowhere to sleep; he often did not know where his next meal was coming from; he was inadequately dressed to endure the rigours of the European winter. He fell ill in the autumn of 1924 and spent over a month in hospital where he was operated on for an intestinal haemorrhage. From the end of 1924 onwards, however, his situation began to improve. The Costa Rican sculptor Max Jiménez gave him the use of his studio. In May 1925 he secured a steady post as secretary in the *Bureau des Grands Journaux ibéro-américains*. Shortly afterwards he became a correspondent of the Lima review *Mundial* and in the following year of *Variedades*. He also contributed articles to *Amauta* and *El Comercio*. This journalistic labour continued till 1930. In these articles Vallejo comments on the European political, social and cultural scene. The articles have little interest in themselves but offer an insight into his thought and its evolution.

Meanwhile Vallejo had formed a wide circle of friends which included the Chilean Vicente Huidobro, the Spaniard Juan Larrea, and the Peruvians Alfonso de Silva, Ernesto and Gonzalo More, Percy Gibson. He lived for a time with a certain Henriette. In 1929 he married Georgette Philippart whom he had known for some time. During this period Vallejo led a bohemian type of existence. Contrary to general belief, he did not cease to write poetry, but composed a number of poems which he intended to be published with the title *Poemas en prosa*.

None the less he felt a profound dissatisfaction with the kind of life he was leading and by 1927–8 this had developed into a grave moral crisis. He came to feel that he had a responsibility towards his unfortunate fellow men and he began to take an interest in social and political questions. He became interested in Marxism, but in the first half of 1928 he fell seriously ill and retired to a small town outside Paris to convalesce. When he recovered he decided to go to Russia to see for himself Marxism at work and he made the trip in October. From 1929 onwards he seems to have written little in the way of poetry, devoting himself to the study of Marxist doctrine. In September 1929 he made a second trip to Russia. By now he had become a convinced Communist and a militant. He took part in demonstrations and clandestine meetings and was arrested by the police on several occasions. At the end of 1930 he was expelled from France because of his political affiliations.

In Madrid Vallejo and his wife lived in extremely difficult

circumstances. None the less, this was a period of intense political and literary activity. He wrote a number of works in prose in which his pen is placed at the service of the proletarian revolution. Of these the short story *Paco Yunque* and the drama *Lock-out* remained unpublished, but he had more success with the novel *Tungsteno* and *Rusia en 1931. Reflexiones al pie del Kremlin.* This last work is of great importance for an understanding of Vallejo's later poetry: in it Vallejo describes the new society that is emerging in Russia and expresses his hopes and ideals for the future. He joined the Spanish Communist Party and taught in one of its cells. In October 1931 he made a third trip to Russia.

In February 1932 Vallejo returned to Paris. Later he obtained a residence permit through the intervention of a friend on condition that he refrain from political activity. He returned with hope and enthusiasm and once again began writing poetry. He continued writing without interruption till the end of 1937. At the same time he wrote a number of works in prose: *Rusia ante el segundo plan quinquenal* (1932); *Colacho hermanos* (1934); *Moscú contra Moscú* (later entitled *Entre las dos orillas corre el río*). These remained unpublished during Vallejo's lifetime. During these years Vallejo had no steady employment and he and his wife lived in considerable hardship.

With the outbreak of the Spanish Civil War Vallejo redoubled his political militancy. He collaborated in the creation of *Comités de Defensa de la República*, wrote propaganda articles, took part in political meetings and taught in workers' cells. He travelled to Spain in December 1936 and in July 1937, on the second occasion to participate in an International Congress of Anti-Fascist Writers. These visits confirmed his fear that the Republic would inevitably be crushed. None the less, he continued working on behalf of the Republic, hoping against hope that the inevitable might be avoided. In the midst of his anxiety and grief he had an outburst of creative activity. In the space of 86 days (3 Sept.– 27 Nov. 1937) he wrote twenty-three poems of *Poemas humanos* and the poems of *España, aparta de mí este cáliz.* Meanwhile the hardships in which he had lived for so long and the exertions to which he had subjected himself had begun to undermine his health, and in March 1938 he fell seriously ill. He was admitted to hospital and he died on 15 April. The doctors were unable to diagnose the cause of death, but Vallejo's wife believes that it was a recurrence of malaria of which he had been a victim in his youth. *Poemas humanos* and *España, aparta de mí este cáliz* were published posthumously in 1939.

II

LOS HERALDOS NEGROS (1919)

Vallejo's first volume contains sixty-nine poems grouped rather arbitrarily in six sections. Only two of these sections—*Nostalgias imperiales* and *Canciones de hogar*—have any real unity and character of their own. *Nostalgias imperiales* initiates a current of nativism and localism in Peruvian poetry. These are poems about the Peruvian countryside, its people, their labours, their diversions, their way of life. The *canciones de hogar* are among the best poems in the collection. Vallejo identified happiness with the integrated and protected world of the home and the family. *Los pasos lejanos* and *A mi hermano Miguel* (p. 96) mark the beginning of the break-up of that world. The latter poem is addressed to the poet's elder brother Miguel, the playmate of his childhood years, who died on 22 August 1915. The effectiveness of the poem proceeds from the opposition of past and present and the alternate superimposition of the one on the other. In the emptiness caused by his brother's death, the poet recalls the childhood games they used to play. So intense is his recollection that he actually re-lives the past: he and his brother are playing at hide-and-seek. But the harsh reality of the present reimposes itself and the game becomes the image of Miguel's death: he has gone permanently into hiding and cannot come out. The climax of the poem is one of great pathos. The poet, an adult, reacts in the present to the situation as he might have done as a child in the past: unable to grasp the fact of his brother's death and accepting literally that he has gone into hiding, he tells him to come out or their mother will be worried. These last lines reveal Vallejo's remarkable genius for capturing the language and mentality of a child.

Los pasos lejanos (p. 95) presents a vision of the paternal home in Santiago. The poet is absent and the other children have also left home, so that the parents are alone. The poem is concentrated on the figures of the father, characterized by his noble and generous heart, and the mother, the image of maternal love. The poem stresses the silence and emptiness of the house: now that the children have grown up and left, the parents feel old and lonely. The son, by his absence, introduces bitterness into the harmony of the family circle. He experiences a sense of guilt and a melancholy tenderness. Separated from his parents in space, he returns to them through his love.

Enereida (p. 97) opens with a vision of the poet's father, 78 years old and near to death. The near-by cemetery at which he has attended so many funerals is a constant reminder that his contemporaries have been dying off one by one and that death is close at hand. It is New Year's morning and the day is sunny, fresh and gay. The opening stanza thus establishes a contrast between the setting and the character, between the freshness and gaiety of the morning and the bleakness of old age, between images of the renewal of life—the morning, the New Year—and images of death—the cemetery, agedness. The father, old and decrepit, unable to go out, lives on memories of the past. He is described as a *víspera*, as someone on the eve of death. But this morning seems to promise an eternal renewal of life. It is the image of the father's love which will live on eternally. The poet finds hope in the approaching death of his father in the conviction that his father's love of his family is an eternal force which will outlive death.

A large proportion of the poems deal with love themes. *Setiembre* and *Heces* refer to a relationship with Zoila Rosa Cuadra in Trujillo in 1917. Vallejo, it seems, was a very difficult lover and the affair broke up after a series of quarrels. In *Setiembre* (p. 87) the poet recalls the sweetness and love the woman brought into his life. He recalls, too, his moods of depression, a depression which he himself never really understood. In these moods he behaved in a domineering and insensitive manner and this eventually killed their love. *Heces* (p. 88) is based on a parallel between the exterior world and the interior world of the poet: rain is falling and the poet's heart is weighed down with grief and he has lost the will to live. The external scene has helped to determine the poet's mood and at the same time is its objective correlative. The poet later turns to the cause of his grief: a relationship that has been ruined because of his egoism and insensitive behaviour. His ingratitude and cruelty spoiled the affair until eventually the woman's dignity put a stop to it. At the end the poem comes back to its starting-point: the rain and his sadness are a reality the poet cannot escape.

The best poems in the volume are those dealing with existential themes. *Los heraldos negros* is a poetry of suffering: of anguish in face of existence. *Espergesia* (p. 98) introduces us to a theme that is to recur in Vallejo's later poetry, that of the outsider, the man whose vision of life is different from that of other people, who has perceived the meaninglessness of life and can no longer feel himself at home in the universe as others do. The opening stanza, which runs throughout the poem as a refrain, indicates that the poet is pursued by a strange fatality which has been hanging over him since birth. In the last analysis this fatality is simply an exteriorization of the poet's obsessive insight which destroys all illusion and isolates him from others. The rest of the poem stresses the poet's isolation and his different vision of life. Others see only his external appearance and his external acts. They understand nothing of his state of soul, of his sense of emptiness, futility and decay. While others see only the surface of things, his insight penetrates deeper and that is why his poetry screeches of desolation and death. Others do not see as he does that the world is plunged in darkness and that such light as there is is sickly, that death is lying in wait for man. In the last stanza the poem comes back to its starting-point: there is no escape from the vicious circle of his suffering. The laconic last line underlines the seriousness of his situation.

The poet finds himself abandoned in an absurd universe, a universe that is illogical, disordered and chaotic. Vallejo sees life as a game of chance in which man is obliged to participate and which he is bound to lose sooner or later. In *La de a mil* (p. 89) the ragged lottery-ticket vendor, who has no control over the good or bad fortune he distributes, is the image of God, who runs the universal lottery governing the lives of men. In *Los dados eternos* (p. 93) life is again presented as a game of chance directed by God. The poet describes himself as a gambler waiting for the throw of the dice to go against him. Life itself is the stake and when he loses, as he must, he must forfeit that life, for it is a game that can end only in death. This theme implies that the universe is given over to disorder and chaos and is ruled by chance.

Vallejo's attitude towards God in *Los heraldos negros* is ambivalent. At times God is considered hostile, cruel and unjust. In *Los dados eternos* (p. 93) God is accused of having irresponsibly created a universe in which man is condemned to suffer, and since God himself is always comfortable, he is insensitive to the suffering he has imposed on his creatures. In *Los anillos fatigados* (p. 94) Vallejo adopts a typically romantic tone of rebellion in face of divine injustice, rising up in protest and pointing an accusing finger at God. Other poems attribute to God the weaknesses of man: he is benevolent and well intentioned but powerless in the face of destiny. Thus, in *Absoluta* (p. 91,) God is seen as being incapable of halting the processes of death and decay. In *La de a mil* (p. 89) God, like the lottery-ticket vendor, is unable to bend destiny to his will and make good fortune fall upon those he wants it to. *Los anillos fatigados* (p. 94) presents suffering as a universal fatality from which even God cannot escape. Eternally bearing all the suffering of the universe on his back, he becomes an object of pity. In *Dios* (p. 95) the poet discovers God through love. Unable to spare his loved one pain, he appreciates how great must be the anguish of God, who, as lover of the universe, is powerless to prevent humanity from suffering.

In Vallejo's world some dark, menacing force of evil pursues man and strikes down blows of misfortune upon him. The poem

Los heraldos negros (p. 87) opens with an affirmation of the existence of such blows. The poet feels himself to be in the presence of something hostile but is unable to understand or explain or even describe these blows. The most he can do is to advance a series of approximations: it is as if God, with all his omnipotence, had directed all his hatred against man; it is as if all the suffering of the past had erupted in the present, so that a lifetime's suffering is experienced in a single moment. In the following stanzas the poet describes physically the effect of these blows and enumerates a series of images in a renewed attempt to describe and explain them. Towards the end of the poem, however, he abandons this attempt and offers us an image of man: a prey to terror, he looks over his shoulder waiting for the next blow to fall. In the course of the poem there is no progression. The poem ends, as it began, with affirmation of the existence of these blows and the poet's inability to understand them, and suffering appears as a vicious circle with no way out. It is significant that this poem should open the book and give it its title: Vallejo clearly intended that it should set the tone for the whole collection. The dark forces of evil hang menacingly over the whole volume.

Man, as he appears in *Los heraldos negros*, is a weak, fragile creature, alone and defenceless in face of a reality which he senses to be hostile and menacing. His condition is hunger, physical and spiritual, and bread is the symbol of the material well-being and spiritual fulfilment he longs for. In this respect the title of *La cena miserable* (p. 93) is significant. The poem poses a number of anguished questions. How long must human suffering last? How long must man wait before his deepest needs and aspirations are fulfilled? The first stanza presents the image of man as a weary traveller on a long, unending road, yearning for the bend where he will at last find his destination and be able to rest at peace, but the cross, symbol of the redemption he longs for, keeps fleeing before him. The second stanza shows humanity seated at a table, waiting, with the bitterness of a child who has woken up at midnight crying with hunger, for the meal that is never served. The world is a valley of tears into which man has been abandoned against his will and in which he feels an exile. He longs for an eternal state, a superior reality where all humanity will be united in love and in which all his appetites and aspirations will be fulfilled. The only one who has eaten well is the dark force ruling human destiny: it stretches out the black spoon of the tomb with which it feeds on man. However, in this poem death is seen as a liberation, for Vallejo seems to believe that the superior reality of which he dreams exists only beyond the tomb. But destiny toys with man, dangling death before his eyes only to snatch it away again, thus prolonging his misery. The dark force of destiny is just as ignorant as man as to when death will strike.

Most of the poems express the poet's anguish in face of existence. In *Absoluta* (p. 91) old clothes, which have the smell and colour of age and death, evoke a winter scene in which the poet feels the world to be decaying and dying around him. He expresses a longing that man might overcome death and achieve a unified state outside time and space in which all humanity would be united in love and the whole universe would vibrate in harmony and unison. But the realities of existence make a mockery of such a longing, for the limitations of man's condition present themselves as insurmountable, and the plenitude of unity is soon poisoned by fragmentation. *Los anillos fatigados* (p. 94) expresses a sense of weariness and defeatism. The poet is a prey to two contradictory emotions. He longs to live happily, to recover the love and protection of the integrated world of his home and family. But at the same time he wishes to die, to have an end to it all, to escape his suffering in death. Life and suffering repeat themselves eternally; thought fills him with anguish; his ideals and his aspirations are constantly frustrated. He experiences a desire not to feel or desire, a longing to abandon everything and to become an inert, unfeeling, inanimate object.

In the midst of his own suffering the poet feels solidarity with the rest of suffering humanity. *El pan nuestro* (p. 90) expresses his indignation at social injustice, at the inhumane conduct of the privileged classes. It is interesting to note that Vallejo conceives society in the evangelical terms of rich and humble. He would like to assume the role of Christ, humbling the rich and distributing bread among the poor. At the same time he experiences guilt, feeling that in some way he is responsible for the suffering of others. He feels that by existing he has deprived others of something that should have belonged to them. He has come into the world to drink the coffee and eat the food that should have gone to others. Thus he feels that he is a thief and that even his body, his very existence, has been robbed from someone else. He would like to beg the forgiveness of all those who suffer, to offer himself to them, to give them his love and out of his love to forge the means of satisfying their necessities.

As a result of this sense of guilt the poet experiences the need to make retribution by doing good to others and, like Christ, he wishes to sacrifice himself for the benefit of his fellow men. *Agape* (p. 89) speaks of the poet's burning desire to give himself to others. But since he has not been asked for anything during the day, he has been unable to give anyone anything. The poem establishes a contrast between the merry passers-by outside and the sad figure of the poet, who is begging to give and to whom no one pays any attention. He feels the need to go out to the door and to shout to the passers-by, but he is rejected, the door is slammed in his face. He can find no one who will ask for or receive his gift. This frustrated longing to give himself makes him feel that he has absorbed something from others, something which he holds uneasily, as if he had robbed it. He begs pardon from Christ for having imperfectly followed his example, for having failed to offer himself in sacrifice for mankind.

None the less, Vallejo does seem to believe at times that man can overcome the misery of his condition through love, that a mankind united by brotherly love will be capable of controlling its destiny. *Líneas* (p. 92) affirms that love will triumph over a blind destiny and give man freedom, unity and fulfilment. The poet expresses the wish that love might vibrate in the soul of every individual, for love is the Christ that will redeem mankind, the embryo that will give birth to a new state of existence. The ideal plane will be attained when each individual becomes a

John the Baptist preparing for the arrival of the Redeemer by spreading the message of redemption. Man will advance along the curve that bends the line of destiny when he bathes himself in purple, when he purifies himself through penance and self-sacrifice, when he gives himself out of love. This concept of redemption through love is to remain a constant in Vallejo's poetry.

When Vallejo began writing Spanish American poetry was dominated by Modernism and by the figure of Rubén Darío. It is not surprising, therefore, that his first volume should show a strongly marked influence of Modernism in general and of Darío and Julio Herrera y Reissig. The influence of Romanticism is also evident; apart from writing a thesis on Romantic poetry, Vallejo was fond of reciting certain Romantics such as the Mexican Manuel Acuña. If on one level the influence of these movements was formal and short-lived, on another it was profound and lasting. The existential anguish that underlies the work of Darío and the Romantics is also characteristic of Vallejo's own poetry. The Romantic theme of a hostile destiny which gratuitously hurls blows of misfortune at man is echoed in the poem *Los heraldos negros*. In *Retablo* Vallejo identifies himself with Darío, the high-priest of poets who "nos lloran el suicidio monótono de Dios", while "la Esfinge preguntona del Desierto" of *Espergesia* is the enigma of existence that caused Darío so much anguish. In a sense Vallejo inherits a spiritual crisis that originated in America with the Romantics and was transmitted to Darío and the Modernists.

Los heraldos negros is essentially a book of transition: in it we see Vallejo gradually free himself from literary influences and move towards a poetry that is a genuine expression of his own personal experience and emotions. The influence of Romanticism is to be noted in poems such as *Los dados eternos* and *La de a mil* which tend to be cerebral and unspontaneous in their conception and in their treatment of existential situations, while there is also a tendency to strike attitudes, as in *Espergesia*. Several poems are purely literary, dealing with themes that are part of the baggage of Modernism. Thus, *Nochebuena,* with its *fête galante* atmosphere, recalls Darío's *Era un aire suave.* The poem is set in moonlit gardens where music and perfume fill the air and shadowy female figures flit past in the darkness. In this refined setting the woman appears as a divine being whose love, like Jesus, offers redemption. There are also reminiscences of Darío in the poet's obsession with the flesh and his subsequent moments of repentance as in *La copa negra* and *Amor prohibido.* The influence of Modernism is also evident in the expression, in a tendency to poeticize reality, dressing it up in pretentious literary language and imagery.

At the same time there is a process of purification as Vallejo gradually breaks loose from these influences. The poems become more authentic, more personal and spontaneous in their inspiration and the poetic emotion is expressed simply and directly. A comparison of the original and definitive versions of the poem *Los heraldos negros* illustrates this point. Lines 11–12 of the original read:

> Son esos rudos golpes las explosiones súbitas
> de alguna almohada de oro que funde un sol maligno[1]

The corrected version reads:

> Esos golpes sangrientos son las crepitaciones
> de algún pan que en la puerta del horno se nos quema.

The correction reveals a passage from pretentious literary imagery to simple imagery drawn from everyday experience. A typical poem of transition is *Heces* where literary language and metaphors still persist alongside a direct, simple, almost colloquial expression. On the other hand, in a poem like *Agape* the language has been stripped of all that is literary and pretentious and is characterized by its utter simplicity. In Vallejo's later poetry simplicity of expression is to remain a characteristic of many poems.

A feature of *Los heraldos negros* is the frequency with which the phrase "Yo no sé" occurs. This points to the fact that the poet finds extreme difficulty in finding an adequate expression for his

[1] Quoted by Espejo, *op. cit.,* p. 179.

states of soul and intuitions of reality, which, moreover, he does not fully understand. Later, in *Trilce* and *Poemas humanos*, Vallejo develops a new poetic language suited to his own needs. In *Los heraldos negros* the first traces are already to be observed. The poet has recourse to neologisms such as *istmarse* and *pajarino*. He changes the grammatical function of a word, using a noun as an adjective—"tan ala, tan salida, tan amor"—and converts a spoken expression into a noun: *yanó*. He incorporates colloquial language into his verse: "Oye, hermano, no tardes en salir. / Bueno? Puede inquietarse mamá." A liking for such *conceptista* devices as antithesis and oxymoron—probably the fruit of his reading of Spanish Golden Age writers—begins to manifest itself: "saboreando un sabor ya sin sabor"; "Hay un vacío . . . que nadie ha de palpar". Vallejo also begins to make use of reiteration and enumeration, techniques which are later to become basic. He insists on words and ideas: "un Bautista que aguaita, aguaita, aguaita". Expressions such as "Hasta cuando . . ." and "Hay ganas . . ." repeat themselves throughout a composition as *leitmotivs*. Enumeration tends to have a reiterative function: "tan suave, / tan ala, tan salida, tan amor"; ". . . aún sigue todo despertando . . . Aún reirás . . . Aún será año nuevo." A characteristic form of enumeration might be called panegyric: it consists in the accumulation of words for the purpose of exaltation: "Día eterno es éste, día ingenuo, infante, / coral, oracional." It is to be noted that this usually involves the use of words whose resonance and musicality reinforce the sense.

In *Los heraldos negros* Vallejo gradually moves away from traditional poetic forms. A large number of poems still conform to traditional patterns of structure, metre and rhyme. Thus *El poeta a su amada* is a sonnet—one of eighteen in the book—written in alexandrines and rhyming abab abab cdc ede. Other poems reveal a transition. In *Absoluta* and *El pan nuestro* the dominant pattern of hendecasyllables and heptasyllables is broken by the introduction of a shorter line. In the first of these poems rhyme is abandoned; the second has stanzas of varying lengths and the rhyme of the early stanzas disappears in the latter part of the poem. The culmination of this process is to be seen in *A mi hermano Miguel* and *Enereida* where rhyme is completely abandoned and the length of the lines and their arrangement in stanzas is determined by the dictates of the poetic emotion. Thus, there is a gradual transition away from forms imposed from without to forms born of the needs of the poetic emotion.

Henceforth the rhythm of the poems is to be internal, and it is to be noted that some of Vallejo's most characteristic techniques, such as reiteration and enumeration, contribute to that rhythm. However, it is interesting to observe that Vallejo retains a certain liking for symmetry and for rhythmic patterns that seem to be derived from Spanish medieval and Golden Age poetry. *La cena miserable* and *Los anillos fatigados*, where the formulae "Hasta cuándo . . ." and "Hay ganas . . ." are repeated six times, are based on parallelisms. In *Espergesia* the first stanza is repeated throughout the poem as a refrain. In *Los heraldos negros* and *Heces* the last lines repeat the first. Such rhythmic patterns are later to become a feature of *Poemas humanos*.

III

TRILCE (1922)

Trilce is a collection of seventy-seven poems, each of which is designated by a Roman numeral. The principal theme of the volume is perhaps the destruction of the happiness of the past. In poem *XXXIII* (p. 109) Vallejo states that he cannot free himself from the misery of his present situation. It is not what life holds in store for him that causes him anguish, but what has been taken away from him and never recovered. Happiness is identified with the past and with people who have gone out of his life—his mother, now dead, and Otilia, now separated from him—and consequently it is irredeemably lost.

A series of poems follow on from the *canciones de hogar* of *Los heraldos negros*, which, as we have seen, signal the beginnings of the break-up of the integrated world of the home and the family. In

Trilce the death of the poet's mother has completed the destruction of that world. Poem *LXI* (p. 119) is a vision of the poet's return to Santiago on the eve of the feast of St. James. He arrives home late at night and calls at the door, but the house is in darkness, the door is closed and no one answers. The home that once rang with the playful laughter of children is now silent. Instead of the loving family circle he expected he finds only an empty house. For Vallejo the home and the family represent the supreme value and this abandoned house is the symbol of the emptiness and desolation of his adult life.

In poem *XLVII* (p. 114) the poet, through his eyelashes as his eyes droop with sleep, has a vision of his childhood home. He recalls his own birth. The foetus is reluctant to leave the womb and to come out into the world, and the newly born baby keeps his eyes lightly closed, arousing the hilarity of the older children. Birth, the expulsion from the warmth and protection of the womb into a cruel world, is man's first misfortune. In the poet's case it foreshadowed another catastrophe, the death of his mother and the break-up of his home. He recalls the candle burning, invoking help and protection for the mother who is giving birth and for the child who, it is hoped, will have a great future. But the poet feels that all that "se va" is slipping away from him: the candle no longer burns and the child grew up to suffering. In his vision he sees his home and family as a reef, a solid rock in the midst of a stormy sea. But now he feels that the rock is disintegrating and becoming submerged. The foundations of his existence have crumbled under his feet. And he is back to the situation of the newly born child, cast out of the warmth and protection of the family into a hostile world. The final image of the child's hands trying to grasp something to hold on to symbolizes the poet's present situation as well as his situation at birth.

In poem *III* (p. 101), which again demonstrates Vallejo's remarkable genius for capturing the language and mentality of a child, the poet relives an incident of his childhood. The parents have gone out, leaving the children at home. Night is falling and the child Vallejo is filled with an irreflexive terror of the menaces lurking in the darkness. He waits impatiently for the grown-ups to return and protect them from danger. His brother and sisters go out into the yard and he calls after them, afraid of being left alone in the house. The poem thus evokes the child's sense of abandonment, loneliness and fear. It is a temporary orphanhood which foreshadows the permanent orphanhood of the adult.

For Vallejo the food of which the family partake in common is the symbol of the love that binds them together, and the table is an altar at which they commune. In poem *XXVIII* (p. 108) the poet eats alone with a terrible sense of privation as he misses all the words and gestures that made up the ritual of the family meal. He has lunch in the house of a friend but cannot swallow the food because everything at the table forms part of a family atmosphere from which he is an outsider and is a reminder that his own home has been broken up. For him life outside the family has no meaning and to eat alone or with strangers is an absurdity.

The whole home revolved around the figure of the poet's mother. Poem *XXIII* (p. 107) opens with an image of her as a warm oven, a provider of life, love and nourishment. She distributed food among her children with all the solemnity of a sacred rite and her *bizcochos* were consecrated hosts providing spiritual as well as material nourishment. These eternal moments represented true time, but now they have given way to the anti-time of the present—the clocks are in pieces and have come to a stop. The invocation to his dead mother evokes all the desolation of adulthood. Now that she is dead, her love can no longer materialize—her bones are flour that cannot be kneaded—and it is death that feeds on the breasts where the child formerly sucked. Before, existence was conferred on him and assured by his mother and needed no justification. Now a cruel world no longer allows him to live life as a right, but demands that he assume responsibility for his existence, that he justify it, that he earn and pay for his presence in the universe. In face of this injustice—he stole his existence from no one—the poet, still an abandoned and defenceless child, appeals to his mother to come to his aid from beyond the tomb.

In the poem just examined the dead mother is powerless to
help her orphaned son. Poem *LXV* (p. 120), on the other hand,
suggests that in some way she transcends death. Here she is
transfigured into a "muerta inmortal", a kind of saint or personal
divinity, and the tone of the composition is solemn and religious.
The poet vows to undertake a pilgrimage to Santiago to receive
his dead mother's blessing and to place himself under her care
and protection. His home is a kind of temple where the familiar
household objects that await him are so many relics animated
with her presence. He makes ready for the pilgrimage by purifying
himself of all egoism and by trying to live up to the legacy of love
and kindness which his mother has bequeathed to him. The sense
of the poem would seem to be that the mother is immortal in that
she lives on in the love that she incarnated and passed on to her
son. Though she is dead, that love still has a validity as the only
force capable of overcoming the absurdity and cruelty of life.
The poet will return to the protection of the womb when other
men adopt and live up to his mother's "fórmula de amor" as he
tries to do. This poem is, therefore, one of the most significant of
the whole volume, for it points to one of the main themes of
Vallejo's later work: the projection on to a universal scale of the
ideal of love inherited from his mother.

The volume also contains a number of love poems, most of
which seem to refer to Vallejo's affair with Otilia. Some are
characterized by their eroticism. Thus poem *LXXI* (p. 121)
describes a moment of unity and fulfilment achieved through the
sexual act. Knowing only too well that such moments are short-
lived, the poet tries to shut out of his mind thoughts of future
unhappiness. In his state of orphanhood he must snatch at
happiness wherever he can find it.

In general, however, the stress is less on the sexual aspect of
love than on woman's maternal nature. Vallejo seems to seek in
Otilia a substitute mother figure. Poem *XXXV* (p. 110) des-
cribes the charms of a lunch which she has spent the morning
preparing for him with loving care. At once sensual and motherly,
she lavishes attentions on him at table. Afterwards she sews a

button on his shirt. He describes her as the "aguja de mis días desgarrados": she repairs not only his clothing but also his battered and shattered life. She sews him to her side, uniting him to her with a protective love that is like the umbilical cord linking mother and child. The image of his dead mother, she promises an ordered and affectionate family life which will re-create the world he has lost.

The happiness that Otilia afforded him was, however, short-lived, and most of the poems refer to the break-up of their affair. Poem *VI* (p. 102) is based on the image of Otilia as a kind of spiritual housekeeper: she tended his spiritual house with her love, and she washed the clothing of his spirit in her veins, in the spring that flows from the heart. But now they have separated he has no one to wash for him and keep his house tidy and everything has fallen into disorder. He feels that none of the things around him really belong to him since they all bear the mark of her love. He wishes that he might at least have the comfort of knowing that one day she will return to bring order and tidiness into the chaos of his life.

In poem *LXXVI* (p. 122) the poet finds himself face to face with an insoluble enigma. He is unable to understand why destiny should have decreed that his affair with Otilia should come to an end. He protests in the name of the woman who loved and who duplicated her personality to identify herself completely with him, whom he treated badly, comporting himself like a stranger, who had no say in the events that led to their separation. He evokes the passion of their bodies, a passion which was never able to reach fruition. Nature intended that they should be united but destiny decreed that they should be separated for ever.

Poem *XXI* (p. 105) is a kind of allegory. In the unending circle in which time continually repeats itself December reappears on the scene. In the course of the year he has completely changed. He is now the gaunt Mr. Twelve, his clothes in shreds, frozen, his nose dripping humiliation. December is the image of the poet himself, shattered by the break-up of his affair with Otilia. He recalls the previous December when their love was at its peak despite the egoism, the jealousies and quarrels that punctuated their affair. The ostrich, a bird that cannot fly and is tied to the earth, is the symbol of Otilia. He loved her, and it is because of her that he has suffered this change.

In poem *XV* (p. 103) the poet, in the room that was the setting for their love, reminisces, recalling all the details that made up their hours of happiness: the corner where they slept, the reading of Daudet, the caresses, the summer days, the comings and goings of Otilia. But all that is in the past and, though he can observe it as a spectacle in his memory, it cannot be recovered. He is brought back to the reality of the present with a start by the noise of doors slamming in the wind. Outside it is dark, rainy and windy and the poet's soul is equally desolate. For these doors shut their love into the darkness of the past and open onto the darkness of a present deprived of love.

A series of poems refer to Vallejo's persecution and imprisonment. In poem *XXII* (p. 106) the poet, in hiding, feels that he is being persecuted by the inhuman representatives of bourgeois society because of his ideals of equality and justice which are feared as a threat to the established order. Outside the sun is shining but it is raining, so that the sun appears as a broken-down lamp and seems to be begging from itself the light it has lost. The sun is the image of the poet's own condition and in a sense his fate is linked to it. The light of his liberty has been darkened and he longs for it to be restored. But the sun is also a symbol of hope, for if he can look forward to the prospect of a full sun which will light up the dark corners of his room, he can equally look forward to the prospect of liberty. He promises that when he is free he will work towards his ideal of a just world in which all men will be united in brotherly love. Thus, despite his persecution, his morale and his ideals remain intact.

In Poem *XVIII* (p. 104) the poet is now in prison and his attention becomes fixed on the four walls of the cell. Whichever way they are looked at they are always four and this unchangeable number is the symbol of inescapability. The confines of the cell torment him, as if he were on an immense rack and his limbs were being torn in four different directions. The thought of the locks and keys of the prison brings to his mind the image of a housekeeper, his mother. If she were there they would be two against the four walls and she would liberate him, just as she always protected him in childhood. In a state of semi-sleep he imagines that the two long walls are dead mothers and the two short ones children being led by the hand along the slopes of the past. These children are the image of his own childhood irremediably lost in the past: the mother can protect and liberate the child but she cannot do the same for the adult. His adulthood is an invalid state since he is alone and abandoned. He is the prisoner of his orphanhood just as much as of the cell. Hence his hand is raised in the air groping for another arm which will look after him in space and time, in his imprisonment and in the orphanhood of his adult years.

In poem *LVIII* (p. 116) reflections and recollections pass in jumbled sequence through the poet's mind as he drowses in the darkness of his prison cell. He recalls scenes from the past: his return to his home in Santiago (st. 3), a conversation with his cell-mate in which the latter gives details of the crime for which he was imprisoned (st. 6, 7). However, in spite of the poem's apparent incoherence there is a dominant preoccupation to which his mind keeps coming back: his sense of responsibility for the suffering of his fellow men. In the second stanza there flashes through his mind a vision in which he fulfils his deep longing to give himself to others, to tend the needs of the destitute. The fourth is dominated by a sense of guilt as the poet feels that this longing will always be frustrated and that what he has to give will never be taken. In the fifth stanza a recollection of the poet's childhood becomes confused with his present vision of his cell-mate: when he was a child eating his fill at his parents' table, unfortunates like his cell-mate were eating with the spoon of suffering that was later to be his. It was not until he himself had experienced suffering that his eyes were opened to the suffering of others. This insensitiveness of the child is reiterated in the eighth and ninth stanzas where the poet recalls that as a child he

used to laugh when his mother prayed for all the unfortunates of
the earth and he used to bully other children. The effectiveness of
these two stanzas resides in the fact that Vallejo re-lives rather
than recollects the past and the adult becomes a child once more.
But it is a child who has awakened to guilt and who has the
adult's consciousness of the reality of evil and suffering. A re-
markable note of pathos is achieved as the child makes an act of
contrition and promises to behave differently in the future.

The starting-point of this poem was the concrete reality of the
cell whose four corners seemed to be huddled in a crouching
position like the prisoners themselves. In the last stanza the poet's
thoughts are interrupted by the noise of a guard stumbling about
in the darkness as he does his rounds, and he is brought back to
the reality of the cell. But this last stanza is intentionally vague
and shadowy. In the course of the poem the cell has been des-
cribed as "lo sólido" and "lo líquido", but now, significantly, it
is "el gas ilimitado". In the poet's mind the concrete reality has
become non-solid and has evaporated. The cell hems in the poet's
body but his mind can go beyond its walls. The real prison is
more intangible, it is life itself, and the ominous noise that is
heard in the darkness is a portent of something hostile and
menacing in existence. Poem *LVIII*, therefore, indicates that,
while many of the poems are based on the poet's own personal
experiences, they are dealing with universal human situations:
just as the cell which encloses the poet is the image of the prison
of life, so, too, the frightened child and the abandoned orphan of
other poems are the image of man, alone and defenceless in a
hostile universe.

As in *Los heraldos negros* a series of poems deal with the misery
and absurdity of the poet's own personal situation and of the
human condition. In poem *LVI* (p. 116) Vallejo states that life
for him has become meaningless and empty: he fumbles his way
through the daily routine like a blind man and the food that
keeps his body alive is tasteless. He reflects that human suffering
is perpetuated from generation to generation: children are born
of love, but it is a love that casts them into a world where their

lot is to suffer and, like God, the parents are powerless to spare their children pain. Life seems to him a pointless absurdity: the oracle that explains the enigma of existence has fallen silent, and like pillars without base or crown, nothing seems to have any foundation or to lead anywhere. Man lives in anguish, striking matches in the darkness in his quest for something which will give a sense to his life. But he never attains the light and life is a barren waste watered only by his tears.

Poem *LX* (p. 118) describes the tedium of a Sunday afternoon. All energy and will have been drained out of the poet. He bears his tedium with patience, but it is the patience of a vegetable, of an inert piece of wood. The day becomes a symbol of the poet's own life: it was born innocent and defenceless and it is being rushed along towards death. The day is leaving him and it is leaving him without dreams or illusions, with a sense of the emptiness and futility of everything. In the final stanza Sunday, the day of rest, becomes the image of the rest of the tomb and the tomb is seen as a great mouth which swallows up man. The poet tires of bearing the tedium and emptiness of life with patience and longs for the repose of death. Life is seen as a Saturday in which man seeks distraction from the futility of existence in pleasure and in so doing engenders children, exiling them into a world not made to their measure and where their lot, too, will be suffering and emptiness. The poet wishes that the Sunday of death might come to put an end to the Saturday of existence.

One of the most important themes of the volume is the attempt to transcend the misery and limitations of the human condition and to attain a meaningful and satisfying existence. Poems of this type tend to revolve around the notion of the absurd as stated in poem *LXXIII*:

Absurdo, sólo tú eres puro.

This extremely complicated notion has two sides to it. It implies first of all that reality is not logical, ordered and harmonious as we normally assume it to be, but illogical, disordered and chaotic. However, it also implies the existence of another reality which is logical, ordered and harmonious but which is outwith our normal experience of logic, order and harmony. To describe both of these "absurd" states Vallejo tends to use the same basic technique of reversing the order of logic as we normally know it.

In this context *Trilce* contains an important numerical symbolism. 1 is the symbol of solitude, abandonment, disharmony: "Y siendo ya la 1" (*XLVII*). 2 is the symbol of harmony, love, unity: "Contra ellas seríamos . . . más dos que nunca" (*XVIII*); "esa pura / que sabía mirar hasta ser 2" (*LXXVI*). The whole volume, in fact, might be said to revolve around a thesis (the integrated world of the past, identified with the home and with Otilia and symbolized by 2) and antithesis (the abandonment and misery of the present, symbolized by 1). The poet strives to arrive at a synthesis, a new ideal state of unity and harmony. Symbol of this synthesis is the number 3: "propensiones de trinidad" (*V*); "en busca de terciario brazo" (*XVIII*). This symbolism would seem to explain the title of the volume. The neologism *Trilce* would seem to be either a reduction of the adjective "tríplice" or a combination of the adjectives "triple" and "dulce".

Poem *XXXVI* (p. 111) opens with an evocation of the sexual act. This moment of erotic pleasure implies the attainment of the impossible, the passage through the eye of a needle and the entry into a new dimension of reality that is unlike existence as we normally know it. In this "absurd" dimension beyond the bounds of logic all limitations are overcome and all contradictions resolved: the circle begins to acquire angles like a square. Male and female rise to a transcendental reality in which they become fused in a new unity. In the second stanza Venus de Milo, with her stunted arm, is the image of man's eternal imperfection and incompleteness. Yet the stunted, or rather ungrown, arm seems to be moving and struggling to grow and become whole. The statue is the image of man's perpetual struggle to transcend the limitations imposed on him by life. Venus de Milo is grasping to achieve a state of imminence, an ideal state which as yet does not exist, a parenthetical third dimension lying between the imperfection of ordinary being and the void of non-being. In the third stanza Vallejo urges us to reject traditional concepts of harmony and symmetry since they impose a false order on life. We must embrace a higher harmony, the illogical, asymmetrical harmony of the absurd, which offers a double security because it resolves all contraries, combining both halves of existence. This harmony can be attained only by facing up to the contradictions and conflicts, the chaos and disorder of life. In the following stanza the poet contrasts his material being with his ideal vision and becomes conscious of the imperfection and absurdity of ordinary existence. He has the absurd sensation that his little finger is superfluous, that it is in the wrong place, that it should not belong to him. This sensation irritates and enrages him and the only escape is to accept that he is in the commonplace, everyday world of temporary and other limitations and to relinquish the ideal as beyond his reach. But Vallejo refuses to retreat and he ends the poem by exhorting us to seek the absurd, asymmetrical ideal dimension by confronting the chaos in which we are orphaned.

In poem *XXXVIII* (p. 112) the glass is a symbol of the "absurd" ideal: it is potential food which can satisfy man's spiritual hunger if approached in the proper fashion. It has to be swallowed by a toothless mouth: to assimilate this higher existence man must avoid disintegrating its essential unity. It is hard and hurts if bitten. It must not be taken by force, because then it refuses to give itself, fights back and inflicts pain. Like a woman, it has to be wooed lovingly and then it becomes transformed, losing its hardness and giving itself. In the third stanza the glass takes on an added significance as a mirror reflecting the poet's condition: when the ideal is unrealized it reveals man's misery to him. It is a sad, dejected, unfulfilled individual. The normal solution would be for it to seek love, to strive to recover a happy past, or to search for a future redemption of an unrealized present. But the glass prefers to suffer rather than accept imperfect solutions and it awaits the grand occasion on which it can give itself totally and completely. In this way it ceases to be an animal: it is not a beast that sates its basic sexual appetite with the first comer, but a superior, spiritual being awaiting "true love". Consequently, it remains unloved, a deprived outcast among "las izquierdas" and "los Menos". But it is to be left in its suffering, for there is something heroic about it and something positive in its privation. For its refusal to accept imperfect solutions permits the possibility of attaining an ideal which will be on the left, outside normal experience, and which will be deprived, i.e. free, of the limitations of ordinary existence. Since the glass is mirroring the poet, the poem expresses his heroic resolve to embrace suffering rather than seek escape in false solutions, his uncompromising determination to await the integral realization of the ideal, his faith in arriving at it.

This attempt to transcend the limitations of life often seems doomed to failure. Poem *V* (p. 102) opens with a vision of a pair of lovers as the union of two personalities flourishing in love. Love opens up a new reality in which all contradictions are resolved in a new unity, symbolized by the trinity. The technique of oxymoron—ends begin, "ohs" of joy emerge from "ays" of sorrow—translates this new unity and expresses the idea of a new reality emerging out of the old and embracing all the heterogeneous elements of life. The poet expresses the wish that this ecstatic moment of unity might be fixed eternally, that it might escape the processes of flux, change and decomposition, that it might not succumb to the transiency that afflicts experiences of the senses. He urges the lovers not to yield to division and change, symbolized by numbers: the number 1 initiates an unending series of numbers, and even 0, which is outside the series, gives rise to 1 and then to the whole series. The last line brings the poem back to its starting-point, the contemplation of the lovers. The poem ends with a sigh and a tone of defeat and regret: unity cannot last.

Poem *LIII* (p. 115) shows man as the prisoner of his human condition. He is caught up in an unending circle of time from which he cannot break free and attain an eternal, timeless existence. As in an auction in which one person tries to outbid another and the price rises, each hour of the clock gives way to the next till 11 comes face to face with 12. Man struggles to reach a deeper reality behind everyday existence, but he comes into collision with his limitations, he cannot break out of the circle which encloses him. The only way to arrive at a spiritually satisfying existence is through an act of religious faith which constructs a bridge loading out of the circle, but Vallejo seems to imply that religion is a farce and that such an act of faith is dishonest. The boundary, symbol of the limits of the human condition, is a baton conducting his life. It is unalterable and it is mobile, so that he cannot skirt it, and the more he struggles the more unsurmountable it seems to become. Powerless in face of his limitations, there is nothing man can do except bite his elbows in frustration.

Other poems are more optimistic. Poem *XLV* (p. 113) evokes a moment of happy fulfilment. The poet is standing on the shore and looking out to sea, which becomes a symbol of life. Normally it is bitter and destructive, but now as its waves lap gently towards him he feels that he is making contact with all that is pure and beautiful in existence. In this moment life is like an unspoilt virgin and the refreshing breeze that passes leaves no salty taste of bitterness. The poet urges us to go outside ourselves and to savour the joys and happiness that life has to offer and which he seems to identify with sexual enjoyment. He hears the surf beating against the shore, like fingers hunting and fumbling for the keys with which to perform a great overture. The sound of the surf seems to echo his own quest for a deeper reality and in the distance he scents the marrow, the essence of existence. The poet envisages the possibility that this quest for the essence of life might bring us face to face with the absurd. The orphaned wing of the day which, since it is only one, cannot fly and is therefore useless is the image of man's incompleteness and limitations and of the absurdity of his condition. But the poet states that to run up against the absurd is no cause for sorrow, for to realize the emptiness and meaninglessness of ordinary existence is the first step towards a new and satisfying reality. To have nothing, to strip oneself of the inessential is to draw nearer the essential. He claims that man can hatch the unborn wing of the night to complement the solitary wing of the day. Thus man will become complete, his limitations will be overcome, flight will become possible, and harmony and unity will be attained.

Poem *LXXVII* (p. 122) is based on the symbolism of rainstorms as the experiences of life. The falling hailstones—rain frozen into stones—are like pearls and they symbolize the poetry the poet has forged out of his experiences. He wishes the rain to continue falling and soaking him, he wishes life to continue holding fresh experiences in store for him. He wants the rain to drench him completely and fears that it will leave part of him still dry; he fears that his experience of life might remain incomplete. He wants the rain to moisten his dry, unused vocal chords. These chords are "incredible" in the sense their function is not that ordinary chords but that of singing a reality beyond the bounds of ordinary experience. He wants to experience and celebrate a new, deeper reality. He states that to sing this new harmony the voice must always be raised in exaltation and suggests by means of a paradox that the way of rising to this ideal state is by descending into the depths of our being. But as yet he has not made contact with this reality and feels his experience to be incomplete. He describes himself as a coast which the sea has not yet reached and he asks the rain to keep falling. It is perhaps significant that this poem should close the volume, for it projects the quest for a fuller existence into the future.

At the same time as the poet seeks to transcend the misery of his condition, he awakes to the suffering of others and identifies himself with the rest of suffering humanity. Several compositions treat the themes of guilt and love that we have already seen in poems *LVII* and *LXV*. Poem *LI* (p. 114) goes back to the world of childhood. The child Vallejo has caused a little girl pain and made her cry. He experiences a sense of guilt and pity for the victim. He explains that it was unintentional and appeals and remonstrates to try to get the other to stop crying. The essence of the poem is that it captures the language and mentality of a child awakening to a consciousness of guilt. In this way childhood foreshadows the adult world.

In poem *XIX* (p. 105) the poet feels hope enter his soul and he begins to think of the possibility of human redemption. He evokes the Nativity and parodies it, presenting it not as the birth of the Son of God, but in terms of natural innocence, symbolized by the excretion of the animals. Vallejo is in fact rejecting the notion of a Redeemer descended from Heaven and postulating the only form of redemption that is conceivable to him: the rebirth of man's natural innocence and goodness. He calls on hope to enter the human soul and to conceive a redeemer just as the spirit of the Holy Ghost entered Mary. He calls on hope to be a herald, an earthly Angel Gabriel announcing the conception of a purely human love in the hearts of men. As Christ was the incarnation of divine love untainted by the earth, Vallejo is thinking of a human love uncontaminated by the divine. Vallejo is here rejecting metaphysical preoccupations in favour of a humanitarianism. Redemption will come when men turn away from the divine and embrace one another in brotherly love. He affirms that the world is in crisis, since the values which previously gave man support have collapsed and the order and harmony which he formerly believed to be there have been disrupted. In view of this man can no longer believe in myths. If he needs myths to live by, then these should be human and earthly ones.

Trilce, then, is a poetry of existential anguish. For Vallejo the happiness of the past has been destroyed and he is trapped in the misery of the present. He desperately strives to break out of the vicious circle of his suffering in two directions. He struggles to find an individual solution to his own personal dilemma, and he moves towards his fellow men. These two aspects come together in his later poetry as he realizes that his own situation is linked to that of others and that redemption can be thought of only in collective terms.

The poems that make up *Trilce* were composed between 1918 and 1922, more than half of them in 1919. The book may be considered to be a part of the world revolution in the arts that took place in the years immediately following the 1914–18 war when avant-garde movements such as Cubism, Dadaism, Surrealism, *Ultraísmo* and *Creacionismo* sprang up in Europe and America. It is important, however, to bear in mind that Vallejo's knowledge of literary developments outside Peru was extremely limited. When he arrived in Lima at the end of 1917 he was acquainted only with the Spanish American Modernists, a few French poets and Whitman. He knew and admired Whitman's *Poemas*, translated by Armando Vasseur (Valencia, 1912), and the North American was possibly a major influence. Such French poets as Verlaine, Mallarmé, Rimbaud, Samain, Jammes, Fort, Maeterlink, Laforgue were known to him only through the selections in Spanish translation included in Enrique Díez Canedo and Fernando Fortún's *Antología de la poesía francesa moderna* (Madrid, 1913). In Lima his knowledge of European literary developments was broadened only by what he could glean from various Spanish reviews which reached Peru. Of these the most important was *Cervantes* which published a number of European avant-garde texts. In the course of 1919 it published an anthology of French poets beginning with Apollinaire; an anthology of *ultraísta* poetry; Vicente Huidobro's *Ecuatorial* and *Halalí*; manifestoes by Picabia and Tzara; a translation of Mallarmé's *Un coup de dés jamais n'abolira le hasard*. Vallejo was obviously influenced by European literary developments. He was influenced in a general sense in that he was encouraged to adopt free verse, to reduce poetry to essentials, to reject external logic for internal logic. He was also influenced in a more tangible way in that he adopted certain specific techniques, mainly various graphic devices. But this influence was not fundamental, for, as will be seen later, the basis of Vallejo's poetry is different from that of other modern poets. It is to be remembered that in *Los heraldos negros* Vallejo began to develop a new literary technique suited to his own needs and in a sense *Trilce* is simply the culmination of this process. To a large extent *Trilce* was written in isolation and independently of literary developments outside Peru, though these did encourage and stimulate Vallejo in his concern to experiment. The transformation of poetic technique that we

find in *Trilce* was not brought about by the influence o
European avant-garde: it would be more accurate to say
Trilce coincides with such movements.

One of the basic things that must be understood about modern
poetry is that expression takes precedence over communication.
The poet is concerned primarily with finding an adequate
expression for his intuition of reality irrespective of whether it is
comprehensible to the reader or not. This leads at times to a
breakdown of communication between poet and reader. In the
case of *Trilce* most of the poems lie between two extremes. On the
one hand, there are poems in which the language is relatively
simple and straightforward and the imagery clear. Such poems
generally refer to concrete experiences—childhood, imprison-
ment, a love affair—and the poet's response to them tends to be
emotional. On the other, there are poems in which the language
is complex and contorted and the imagery hermetic. These
generally refer to the anguish of the poet's condition and are
intellectual and abstract in character. In a number of poems both
expressions exist side by side. Most poems contain obscurities.
Occasionally a poem is completely incomprehensible. This is the
case of poem *XXV* which, to date, has baffled all of Vallejo's
critics. The first stanza gives some idea of its hermeticism:

> Alfan alfiles a adherirse
> a las junturas, al fondo, a los testuces,
> al sobrelecho de los numeradores a pie.
> Alfiles y caudillos de lupinas parvas.

Happily this poem is not typical.

In common with other avant-garde poets Vallejo tends to
reduce poetry to essentials, eliminating the anecdotic and descrip-
tive, cutting out adjectives whose function is purely decorative,
and suppressing intermediate phrases and connectives. Conse-
quently, his poetry is remarkably elliptic and concentrated. This
is immediately noticeable on a rather obvious plane in the
suppression of connectives—"Es posible me persigan" (p. 106)—
and punctuation marks, though it is not done systematically. In
general, however, this extreme concentration goes much deeper

and is less easy to detect. In the expression "heme, de quien yo penda" (p. 107) the antecedent of the relative pronoun is simply implied in the invocation to the sun: the phrase could be reconstructed as "heme, oh sol, de quien yo penda". Moreover, by employing the verb in the subjunctive, and not in the indicative as would have been expected, Vallejo implies not that his fate is linked to that of the sun but that it might be or that he would like it to be. Thus by the simple use of a subjunctive he avoids a cumbersome construction. Similarly, the expression "los mayores siempre delanteros / dejándose en casa" (p. 101)—"the grownups who are always quick to leave us behind"—concentrates an awkward relative clause in an adjective and a gerund.

This is a poetry that suggests indirectly rather than states directly and in this respect a comparison of two versions of the same poem is revealing. The first version of poem *LXI* concludes:

> . . . mi caballo
> cansado empieza a cabecear, también
> a cabecear; y así entre sueños hallo
> que el animal, a cada venia, dice
> que todo está muy bien, pero qué bien![1]

The definitive version reads:

> mi caballo acaba fatigado por cabecear
> a su vez, y entre sueños, a cada venia, dice
> que está bien, que todo está muy bien.

The first version explains that both horse and poet are dozing and that it is in a dream that he sees the horse's head nodding, while in the second version this is merely implied. There is even a certain ambiguity since the dreams seem to be the horse's as well as the poet's and the impression is thus conveyed that the horse shares the poet's emotion. It would seem that this extreme concentration is intended to give the poem greater force and impact and to leave more free-play for the reader's imagination.

Like other modern poets Vallejo abandons external logic for internal logic. A poem has two levels: the internal (the poetic emotion) and the external (the representation of that emotion).

[1] Quoted by Espejo Asturrizaga, *op. cit.*, p. 192.

The modern poem differs from the traditional poem in that, whereas the latter is logical and coherent on both levels, the logic and coherence of the former is that of the poetic emotion and there is no concern that its external representation should be logical and coherent. Hence the relationship between the two levels is not always logically apparent. Often there is no direct reference to the stimulus of the poetic emotion and instead it is reduced to an image that symbolizes its emotional import. Nor is the emotion explained but is conveyed to us by the imagery. Thus, while the starting-point of poem *XXXVI* (p. 111) is the sexual act, this is not immediately obvious: "Pugnamos ensartarnos por un ojo de aguja, / enfrentados, a las ganadas." What is conveyed to us is the physical and emotional effort and tension involved.

Moreover, the images the poet employs to express his emotion often have no relation with one another on the objective plane but achieve unity and coherence through the underlying poetic emotion they represent. Externally the third line of the same poem bears no relation to the first two: "Amoniácase casi el cuarto ángulo del círculo." But on the internal level the relationship is perfectly logical: through love it is possible to glimpse a new dimension of reality in which everyday concepts are obsolete. Similarly, the second stanza enumerates four images which have nothing in common externally but which all reinforce the central image of the stunted arm struggling to grow: ". . . verdeantes guijarros gagos, / ortivos nautilos, aunes que gatean / recién, vísperas inmortales." Cobblestones turning green as they become overgrown with moss and stuttering like young children learning to speak; cephalopods rising from the sea like a celestial body from behind the horizon; potentialities which have only just begun to realize themselves and which crawl like babies; eves perpetually on the brink of a new day: all represent the striving to transcend limitations and to attain new life.

The rejection of external logic means, too, that a poem follows the train of the poet's thoughts and emotions rather than an artificial order imposed from outside by the reason. Thus in a poem like *XXXVI* the stanzas, rather than follow on logically from one another, are separate units. Each corresponds to a different moment of the poet's intuition and a central thread— the ideal state of harmony and unity to which the poet aspires— gives the poem an underlying unity.

From what has been said, it is obvious that Vallejo's poetry only appears to be incoherent on the surface and that it is perfectly coherent in its own way. It is to be emphasized that the "incoherence" of the poems does not mean that they were written under the impulse of inspiration nor that they are disorganized. Nothing could be further from the truth: Vallejo constantly revised, corrected and elaborated his poems and *Trilce* is the fruit of the patient labour of a dedicated artist.

Vallejo stands apart from other modern poets in that the basis of his poetry is not imagery but language, and his originality springs from his original use of language. It has been said that Vallejo writes as if he were unaware of the existence of language and syntax and creates his own. In this he has been compared to a child who is only beginning to speak and who makes up his own words and structures to express what he has to say. Bearing in mind that he is not a stammering child but an intelligent and dedicated artist laboriously evolving a technique, there is a great deal of truth in this view of Vallejo. Frequently these distortions and abuses are a direct consequence of his concern for concentration. Thus he consistently employs the gerund with the value of a relative clause: "Son dos puertas abriéndose cerrándose" (p. 104) = "Son dos puertas que se abren y se cierran". He frequently has recourse to catachresis, the improper use of a word to qualify another: "bromurados declives" (p. 104); "núbil campaña" (p. 110); "dedos pancreáticos" (p. 110); "se ha calzado todas sus diferencias" (p. 106). Another common device is the use of possessive and indefinite adjectives, numerals and even nouns as qualifying adjectives: "todas no están *mías*" (p. 103); "*poca* y harta y pálida" (p. 103); "más *dos* que nunca" (p. 104); "ló más *piedra*" (p. 105). Other abuses are less systematic, more arbitrary and certainly much more disconcerting.

In the expression "de brindarse" (p. 112) "de" has the sense of "para". In the phrase "Es posible me persigan hasta cuatro / magistrados vuelto" (p. 106) "vuelto" fulfils the function of an adverbial clause of time ("cuando vuelva" or "cuando haya vuelto": "when I've returned from hiding"). One of the most disconcerting examples is the following: "ni padre que, en el facundo ofertorio / de los choclos, pregunte para su tardanza / de imagen, por los broches mayores del sonido" (p. 108). The reader is perplexed by the unusual use of the prepositions "para" and "por" and of the noun "imagen". "Para" means "the reason for"; "por" is the equivalent of "mediante"; "imagen" has the sense of the verb "aparecer"; the father asks at the top of his voice why the *choclos* are so late in appearing on the table. Examples such as this are relatively few and the sense can usually be deduced from the general tone and context.

For Vallejo words are not simply names to designate objects or qualities or actions but have magical properties of association. He chooses words not merely for what they represent but also for the connotations they carry with them. In the phrase "la más torionda de las justas" (p. 112), for example, the adjective signifies passionate but also brings in associations of animals in heat. In the expression "ahito de felicidad" (p. 116) the adjective means surfeited, but also implies the idea of indigestion. In the phrase "Es posible me juzguen pedro" (p. 106) "pedro" has at least four connotations: a case of mistaken identity; an ordinary insignificant person; a traitor; its etymological meaning of stone. Equally Vallejo often selects words for their acoustic associations. Thus the sense of expressions such as "en tordillo retinte de porcelana" (p. 108), "apura . . . aprisa . . . apronta!" (p. 117), "de correa a correhuela" (p. 120) is reinforced and enrichened by alliteration and onomatopoeia.

Everyday spoken language is particularly rich in overtones and finds its place in Vallejo's poetry. Spoken expressions are sometimes used as nouns: "ohs de ayes" (p. 102); "tanto qué será de mí" (p. 103). More commonly complete phrases are incorporated directly into his verse: "Se ha puesto el gallo incierto, hombre" (p. 105); "Así, qué gracia!" (p. 109); "suelta el mirlo" (p. 111). In his concern to reproduce spoken language Vallejo at times deliberately incurs grammatical errors: "¡el mío es más bonito de todos !" (p. 101). Poems such as *III* and *LI*, which are dramatizations of childhood incidents, are based entirely on the reproduction of spoken language.

One of the great problems of language is that words tend to become drained of their significance by social usage. Vallejo gets round this difficulty in various ways. In some cases he endows ordinary words with fresh significance. Thus "impar" (p. 112), "izquierdas" (p. 113), and "Menos" (p. 113) come to designate that which is outside our normal concept of order. They have both positive and negative implications. The "impar" is at once the disharmony of ordinary existence and the asymmetrical "absurd" ideal state. The "izquierdas" are outsiders and pariahs and the "Menos" are deprived, but they are so because they them-selves reject ordinary existence in their longing for transcendental fulfilment. Alternatively, Vallejo has recourse to archaisms such as "yantar" (p. 109), "tahona estuosa" (p. 107), "della" (p. 122), or technical terms drawn from the various branches of the arts and sciences, law, mathematics, etc.: "pancreático" (p. 110), "bicardiaco" (p. 102), "cotiledones" (p. 102), "pistilo" (p. 110), "erogar" (p. 117), "equis" (p. 122), etc. Generally such words do not merely designate but also carry connotations: the archaisms quoted designate the family meal, the mother and the lover re-spectively but also endow them with a certain majesty and place them on a mythical plane; "equis" signifies enigma but brings in associations of all the unknown quantities of mathematics.

Vallejo also creates new words of his own. Sometimes this means changing the grammatical function of a word: "aunes que gatean" (p. 112); "todaviiza" (p. 111). In some cases he employs a neologism where an equivalent already exists and it would seem that his concern is simply to avoid commonplace terms in order to give special significance to the experience he is describing. Thus "inacorde" is used instead of "discorde" (p. 109), "excre-mentido" instead of "excrementado" (p. 105), "enmendatura" instead of "enmendadura" (p. 106). In other cases the neologism carries implications that the nearest equivalent does not have. "Oberturar" (p. 102) means to open and refers to the opening of the wings of the petrels and to the opening up of a new dimension of reality, but it also brings in connotations of a musical overture. "Fratesado" (p. 103) combines the words "fratasado" (smoothed with a trowel) and "fraternal" and has the sense of sealed with love. "Pupilar" (p. 104) means to watch over but also implies the duties of a ward with regards to an orphan.

The originality and force of Vallejo's language proceeds in large part from the use of various conceptual devices. The reader comes across occasional plays on words: "cómo quedamos de tan quedarnos" (p. 105). The most characteristic of these devices bring opposites together: antithesis, oxymoron and paradox. Antithesis is the contrast of ideas expressed by a parallelism of contrasting terms: "(si) a hablarme llegas masticando hielo, / mastiquemos brasas" (p. 105). Oxymoron is the conjunction of seeming contradictions: "hembra se continúa el macho" (p. 111); "finales que comienzan" (p. 102); "en son de no ser escuchado" (p. 102). Oxymoron often involves paradox, an apparent absurdity conflicting with preconceived notions of what is reasonable or possible: "El traje que vestí mañana" (p. 102); "el cuarto ángulo del círculo" (p. 111); "me he sentado / a caminar" (p. 103); "¿No subimos acaso para abajo?" (p. 123). Such devices shock the reader into seeing reality in a different way. As we have already seen, they often serve to translate the absurdity of reality as we know it or a deeper reality beyond the bounds of everyday logic. Though Vallejo's use of these devices is highly personal, they are reminiscent of Spanish writers of the Golden Age and seem to point in particular to the influence of Quevedo. This is an important reminder that while Vallejo's poetry is completely modern and revolutionary in its expression, it has roots in the Spanish classical tradition.

In *Trilce* Vallejo also seeks to increase the expressiveness of language by stressing words in various ways. Sometimes he breaks normal syntactic patterns: in the expressions "el sin luz amor"

(p. 105) and "torna diciembre qué cambiado" (p. 105) the words "sin luz" and "cambiado" are thrown into relief by their unusual positioning. Emphasis is also the function of various graphic devices, of which the most common is the use of capitals: "que no brinda la / MADRE" (p. 109); "¡ CÓMO NO VA A PODER !" (p. 103); "el placer que nos DestieRRa" (p. 118). On occasions he isolates words from a line:

> diciembre con sus 31 pieles rotas,
>> el pobre diablo. (p. 105)

Or he separates words by long spaces: "sombra   a   sombra" (p. 104). In other poems, not included in this anthology, Vallejo is much more daring in his use of graphic devices. In poem *LXVIII*, for example, the expression "a toda asta" is written vertically, while in *XIII* "estruendo mudo" is written in reverse.

Free verse, which permits the poet to end a line wherever he wishes, is also exploited by Vallejo for the purpose of emphasis. A simple example is the phrase "Es el rincón / amado" (p. 103). Normally noun and adjective would go together as a group but by placing the noun at the end of one line and the adjective at the beginning of the next the poet emphasizes each of them individually. The effectiveness of this technique resides not merely in the positioning but also in that there is a simultaneous pause and enjambment: there is a momentary poetic pause at the end of the first line, but syntactically there is an enjambment so that we are immediately brought face to face with the adjective. At times the purpose of this technique is to emphasize only the second term by creating a pause before it: "no he tenido / madre" (p. 108). Vallejo employs this technique systematically, and he even carries it to the extreme of splitting a word: "boca ve- / nidera" (p. 113). The poet is here referring to an ideal future mouth which will be capable of swallowing glass. By underlining the particle "ve-" he gives the adjective connotations of vision: the mouth will have the perspicacity to see the transparent glass for what it potentially is.

One of Vallejo's basic techniques is reiteration. Much of the force of his poetry comes from his tendency to insist again and again on words and ideas. This may involve a simple repetition: "la vaca inocente / y el inocente asno y el gallo inocente" (p. 105); "aquí me tienes, / aquí me tienes" (p. 106). More commonly a word or phrase is reinforced or elaborated by another: "mudas equis" (p. 122); "fratesadas, selladas" (p. 103); "que no se juntan, / que no se alcanzan" (p. 122); "en sus venas otilinas, en el chorro de su corazón" (p. 102). Equally common are enumerations with a reiterative function: "satisfecha, capulí . . ., dichosa" (p. 103); "O sin madre, sin amada, sin porfía" (p. 109); "se ajan, / se doblan, se harapan" (p. 117); "y no he tenido / madre, ni súplica, ni sírvete, ni agua, / ni padre" (p. 108). Reiteration may also take the form of the enumeration of a series of images referring to a central idea: "Oberturan / desde él petreles, propensiones de trinidad, / finales que comienzan, ohs de ayes" (p. 102). It may involve the repetition of a grammatical formula: "Estoy cribando . . . Estoy ejeando . . . estoy plasmando . . ." (p. 120); "En nombre de esa pura . . . En nombre de que . . . En nombre della . . ." (p. 122). Some poems are built around certain key words which echo one another throughout the composition. Thus poem *XXIII* (p. 107) is based on words referring to food and eating: "Tahona . . . bizcochos . . . yema . . . gorgas . . . hostias . . . alvéolo . . . migaja . . . harina . . . amasar . . . molar . . . encía . . . lácteo hoyuelo."

Like other modern poets, Vallejo abandons traditional verse forms for free verse. The rhythm of traditional verse tends to be arbitrary and mechanical, since it is imposed from without and is determined by factors which are purely formal—number of syllables, rhyme, distribution of accents, etc. This means that a line of traditional poetry is a rhythmic unit independent of units of sense. Modern poetry, on the other hand, follows the rhythm of the poetic emotion and its rhythmical units correspond to units of sense. Free verse, therefore, does not imply the abandonment of rhythm but an internal rhythm born of the poetic emotion. Moreover, certain of Vallejo's techniques—the reproduction of spoken language, enumeration, reiteration—have a rhythm of their own. In addition, Vallejo displays a liking for certain types of line which are rhythmical in themselves. Of these the most frequent are binary lines: "enfrentados, a las ganadas" (p. 111); "finales que comienzan, ohs de ayes" (p. 102); "el sin luz amor, el sin cielo" (p. 105). Also common are parallel lines: "ya no hay donde bajar, / ya no hay donde subir" (p. 105); "Fósforo y fósforo en la oscuridad, / lágrima y lágrima en la polvareda" (p. 116). Thus, though at first sight the poems of *Trilce* may seem disjointed, they are remarkably rhythmical.

IV

POEMAS HUMANOS/ESPAÑA, APARTA DE MÍ ESTE CÁLIZ (1939)

Published posthumously in 1939, *Poemas humanos* gathered together some ninety-odd poems written during Vallejo's fifteen years in Europe, most of them in the years 1936–7. These included a number of prose poems, composed between 1923 and 1929, and which, Georgette de Vallejo has revealed, the poet intended to be published as a separate book entitled *Poemas en prosa*. In a sense these compositions represent a transition between *Trilce* and *Poemas humanos* and should be studied separately, but I have preferred to follow the format of the first edition for reasons of convenience and to treat them as part of *Poemas humanos* since I believe that all of Vallejo's European production should be considered as a whole. Also published in the same volume were the fifteen poems on the Spanish Civil War that make up the collection *España, aparta de mí este cáliz*.[1] *Poemas humanos* and *España* . . . must be examined together since they constitute complementary works.

In *Trilce* we have seen Vallejo struggle to break out of the vicious circle of his anguish and to arrive at a personal solution to his existential misery. At the same time we have seen him identify himself with the suffering of others. Subsequently these two aspects of his work come together. He becomes more and more aware of

[1] Henceforth this title will be abbreviated to *España* . . .

the misery of his fellow men and of the injustice of society. At the same time he comes to realize that it is useless to think in personal terms since his situation is linked to that of others and that a collective solution is needed. This evolution leads him to embrace Communism: he becomes convinced that the salvation of man lies in the Revolution and in the creation of a Communist society.

In *Un hombre pasa* . . . (p. 146) Vallejo implies that all purely literary, artistic or intellectual preoccupations are dishonest evasions and that the intellectual and the artist must take account of all the multiple forms of human suffering—poverty, hunger, violence, injustice. Here, by implication, he is expressing the belief that literature should be involved in that the artist should concern himself with all aspects of reality. However, he does not confuse artistic involvement with political involvement. Elsewhere he states clearly that, while his work might have political implications, he cannot subordinate his artistic liberty to any political cause: ". . . en mi calidad de artista, no acepto ninguna consigna o propósito, propio o extraño, que aún respaldándose de la mejor buena intención, someta mi libertad estética al servicio de tal o cual propaganda política . . . como artista, no está en manos de nadie ni en las mías, el controlar los alcances políticos que pueden ocultarse en mis poemas."[1] While these words were written before Vallejo's adherence to Communism and seem to be contradicted in *El Tungsteno*, where one of the characters affirms that the intellectual must place himself unreservedly at the service of the masses, his poetry remains faithful to this position. Vallejo does not write in function of his Communism and his verse does not expound Marxist–Leninist propaganda. His final poetic works are existential rather than social and political. It is true that many poems deal with the misery and destitution of the underprivileged, the pariahs and oppressed of capitalist society, or sing of the Revolution and the Spanish Civil War. But for Vallejo the victims of society are also the victims of life and the Civil War is not simply a struggle against Fascism but a symbol of man's struggle to create an ideal world. In the Revolution

[1] 'Literatura proletaria', *Mundial*, Lima, 21 Sept. 1928.

Vallejo sees not only the possibility of a change in the social structure but of an eventual transformation of the conditions of life.

If Communism gave a direction to Vallejo's life and a goal towards which to work, it did not dramatically solve his existential problems. These still remain and constitute the subject matter of most of *Poemas humanos*, though a significant evolution is that he is now much more concerned with the condition of man and not simply with his own personal situation. What Communism did hold out for him was the prospect of a future world in which the conditions of life would be completely transformed, though not in the poet's lifetime. Thus Vallejo's final works move between two poles, the absurd world of the present and an ideal world of the future. On the one hand, most of *Poemas humanos* expresses the poet's anguish, the misery of the human condition, the absurdity of existence; on the other, *España . . .* and a number of compositions from *Poemas humanos* prophesy a future in which man will dominate nature and control his destiny.

Poemas humanos consists mainly of monologues in which the poet reflects on the absurdity of existence. *Altura y pelos* (p. 154) is based on an opposition between the poet and other men. Vallejo builds up a picture of ordinary life with its routine and its order, with its assumptions of meaning, purpose, usefulness. Men lead an empty, superficial existence which they believe to be meaningful. They have names and they play with the cat: they are insignificant little people doing insignificant little things, but they believe themselves important and they believe that what they are doing is important. The poet affirms his inability to participate in such a routine. He has been born, he exists, but nothing more: all that he knows is existence, stripped of purpose, aim or significance. He affirms his anguish, his loneliness, the absolute nakedness of his existence, but it is implied that his anguish is in some way superior to the unconsciousness of other men, for he has perceived the meaninglessness of the routine that they lead.

Existe un mutilado . . . (p. 157) introduces us to a man who is deformed, the victim not of an accident or of an act of violence but of something inherent in life itself. He is, in fact, a man who has become conscious of the meaninglessness of life and his deformation is the exterior mark of his sense of unfulfilment and incompleteness. It is significant that it is the man's face and head that have been corroded, for these are the centre of the brain and the other faculties. His deformation is not only the badge of his suffering, but also a sign that he has lost or never possessed the faculties to discern a meaningful pattern in existence.

In an absurd world the poet, aspiring to unity, finds himself surrounded by chaos, disorder, division. To translate this disorder and chaos Vallejo employs two basic techniques. One is to break with the norms of logic, reversing the order we normally assume to be present in the universe. In *Los nueve monstruos* (p. 134) he explains that experience of suffering opens our eyes to the chaos around us. Then we see things in reverse: water flows vertically, eyes are seen instead of seeing, ears emit noises instead of hearing them. The second technique is much more common: the juxtaposition of opposites. Vallejo was obsessed by the contradictions inherent in life, with the fact that day cannot exist without night, heat without cold, good without bad, life without death, etc. This obsession manifests itself in the form of verbal oppositions. Thus *¿ Qué me da . . . ?* (p. 154) is made up of couplets in which the last term of the second line opposes the last term of the first. Those stanzas which do not conform exactly to this pattern contain some element of opposition within them. In this way the poem opposes eternity and time, life and death, body and soul, the individual and his fellow men, aspiration and reality, sorrow and joy. In the last line the poet states that he is neither alive nor dead. More exactly, he is alive in so far as he is breathing, but he is dead in that he does not live fully. He indicates, too, that these contradictions have ceased to matter to him: in an absurd world nothing matters, nothing has any importance.

An important aspect of the absurd is the conflict between aspiration and reality, the gulf between man's longings and ideals and his inability to attain them. The poet longs for a harmonious and unified existence, a way of life that will be complete and fulfilling and which will satisfy his deepest needs. The most he can achieve, however, are a few isolated moments of personal fulfilment. *Al fin, un monte* . . . (p. 129) is one of the few poems to describe such a moment. The poet emerges from the depths of unfulfilment and suffering and reaches the hilltop of plenitude. The hill, the reward for the frustrations and misery of dragging oneself through the depths, stands on top of veins of golden silver: silver, the imperfect, has been purified and converted into gold. For a long time he found no outlet for his energies, no fulfilment for his longings: it was as if the valves which should have afforded them an outlet had been blocked up. But now all his forces, all his energies and longings, burst forth towards this goal and his whole being—feet, skin, fingers—vibrates in unison. As he hugs himself with joy, the poet feels so full of happiness that he is in danger of bursting unless he gives voice to it. This hill has been the source of prayers of longing and tears of frustration, and it is scaled only by great effort and striving. But now that he has reached the top it seems low and easily accessible, and there opens before his eyes a fairyland panorama of towers and palaces. He then goes on to evoke the landscape of the Peruvian *sierra*, the world he knew as a child: this moment of fulfilment seems to him to reproduce the happiness of childhood.

These moments, however, are rare and short-lived. In general the poet's aspirations are frustrated by the realities of existence. All his efforts to be happy end in failure. Again and again he runs up against the limitations of his human condition. *Nómina de huesos* (p. 157) is a parable of man's situation. By its form it recalls Abraham's intercession on behalf of the city of Sodom (Genesis xviii. 23–33): man is asked to perform a number of tasks but proves incapable of doing so. These tasks are examples of his limitations, limitations which prevent him from realizing his ideals and which condemn him to a life that is empty and meaningless. The fact that these are simple, everyday tasks underlines how limited are man's powers. These tasks, however, may be interpreted on a symbolic level: thus the impossibility of grouping together similar men symbolizes man's inability to break out of the prison of his isolation, while the impossibility of comparing him with himself symbolizes his inability to harmonize the conflicting parts of his nature.

The frustration of his aspirations by the realities of existence leads the poet to complete disillusionment with regards to life. In *¡ Y si después de tantas palabras . . . !* (p. 155) words and birds' wings are the symbols of man's aspirations. For centuries men have discussed, argued, written books, elaborated doctrines, searching for the eternal word that would give life a transcendental meaning; from the beginning of time birds have launched themselves into the air and climbed towards the heavens, as though in search of some ideal resting place. But it seems that man is never to find the eternal word and that the bird is never to reach its ideal destination. The first stanza is based on a conditional: if the image of an ideal existence that man carries within him does not correspond to a really existent state or to a state capable of attainment, then there is no point to life. And if this is the case, it would be better that everything come to an end rather than that man go on living in a world not made to his measure. The rest of the poem follows in the same vein, but in the last stanza the poet recognizes that others might draw a different conclusion from his proposition: they might claim that his vision is subjective, that he is a person who has suffered personal misfortune and that his personal grief leads him to see everything in black. He recognizes that most men will never understand his position and that it is impossible to argue with such people. The last stanza is a satire of those who refuse to open their eyes to the absurdity of existence.

Of the various contradictions in life the greatest is man himself, "el bimano, el muy bruto, el muy filósofo". For Vallejo part of the tragedy of man is that he aspires to an integrated, unified existence, but finds himself divided in a state of inner discord. There is in man an essential duality: the divergent parts of his nature are in constant conflict and are never able to fuse together and harmonize. Basically, this is a conflict between that part of man which longs to be free to develop its potentialities and to forge an existence that will be spiritually fulfilling, and that part of him which is determined and limited by forces outside his control: heredity, environment, education, physical and psychological needs. Generally, however, it is presented in terms of the tension between man's spiritual nature and the physical. In accordance with Darwin's theory of evolution Vallejo considers man to be little more than an advanced animal species. Hence he employs the names of animals to designate man: "antropoide", "mono", "mamífero", "paquidermo", "cetáceo", "kanguro", "jumento", "conejo", "elefante". Hence, too, he places great insistence on the human organism and on the role it plays in the life of man. *Poemas humanos* contains ninety-odd different nouns referring to the human anatomy. What emerges is a picture of man dominated by bodily appetites and functions. Man, then, is an animal, but he is also a spiritual being. If he were simply an animal he would enjoy the uncomplicated existence of an unthinking beast. He is an animal who thinks and feels and aspires to rise above his animal state. His greatest suffering springs from his inability to do so. He aspires to an existence which will fulfil his deepest spiritual needs but the limitations of his physical nature deny him such fulfilment.

In *Epístola a los transeúntes* (p. 126) the poet wakes up to resume the elemental routine that is his life. Night and day, in action or at rest, he is an animal, as insignificant as a rabbit and as cumbersome as an elephant. He contemplates his body and reflects that it is an inert weight anchoring him to the ground and preventing him from reaching the heights. The body completely swamps the spiritual and the shattered lamp of his ideals has been swallowed up by his stomach. The formula on which the poem is based recalls the words of Christ: "... this is my body ... this is my blood ..." (Mark iv. 22–24), but there is an irony in this implicit comparison between Christ's divine nature and the human animal completely dominated by physical needs and functions.

The title of *El alma que sufrió de ser su cuerpo* (p. 126) is significant: the soul suffers because it has to assume bodily form, because it is imprisoned within the body. Man is an ape living in spiritual darkness. Like a moth around a candle, man circles around the sun, symbol of the ideal. The ideal attracts him irresistibly but he can never reach it. He clings to his soul, striving to achieve a spiritual existence. He extends his extremities as if trying to fly but it is obvious that his physical limitations make flight impossible. He cannot escape the demands of his body and even in the midst of spiritual strivings he has to attend to his physical needs, such as tidying his dress. Man is imprisoned in his liberty: he has the illusion of being free but in reality he is a prisoner of himself, enclosed within the limitations of his human condition. He is the slave of his body—symbolized by the Greek hero Hercules—which, unlike the spirit, is free in that it refuses to be dominated by the spirit. Man's limited powers of thought—to count up to two is a painful effort for him—increases his anguish by making him aware of the number two, of the duality from which he cannot escape.

An essential feature of *Poemas humanos* is the attempt to surmount the state of duality to which man is condemned. In *Palmas y guitarra* (p. 148) Vallejo speaks of transcending physical limitations and attaining spiritual plenitude through the act of love. He invites the woman to come with her two personalities to him with his two personalities, and to unite with him in the act of love. Love is seen as a dark and tremulous night, since in it the lovers, quivering with passion, experience the annihilation of their individual personalities. But it is a night that is full of light, since it opens on to another plane of reality in which the lovers can escape from their physical existence into the spiritual. In the act of love the woman will not only be united with the poet but she will transcend her everyday personality and life as it is normally lived, thus discovering her true essence and reaching a higher plane of existence where her spiritual needs will be satisfied. In the second stanza a series of paradoxes—in coming to the poet, the woman is coming to herself; through an act which is part of the normal course of life, the lovers go above and beyond the normal; the union of the lovers is a parting; learning is ignorance

alongside the true knowledge attained through love—indicate
that there exists a plane of reality beyond the limits of contradic-
tion. The act of love is thus seen as a journey to another world on
which the lover's spiritual personalities embark, leaving their
physical personalities behind in this world. At the end of the
composition the significance of the title becomes apparent. Music
is the symbol of transportation: the poet asks the woman to allow
her soul to become enraptured and to transport him to another
plane of existence. Thus their two souls will part together,
leaving their bodies behind.

Palmas y guitarra speaks of the possibility of transcending
duality through love, but few poems offer any evidence of the
actual attainment of unity. What emerges is rather a conviction
that duality is permanent and irremediable. In this sense the
chaos and fragmentation of life is embodied in man himself.

The absurd also manifests itself in the inexplicable presence of
evil and suffering in the universe. One of the blows of misfortune
of which Vallejo had spoken in *Los heraldos negros* constitutes the
theme of *Hoy le ha entrado una astilla* . . . (p. 142): a terrible blow
has befallen a poor lady. This blow is expressed by the image of
a splinter piercing her. The immense and anonymous force of
evil, apparently far off, has struck down on the lady when she
least expected it, pursuing her and overtaking her with one vast
stride. Misfortune has introduced havoc into her life, converting
everything into a source of suffering. Suffering undermines the
whole basis of her existence: it destroys all her faith, all her com-
forting beliefs, and her life loses its direction. The poet insists on
the enormity of the poor lady's pain and concludes the poem with
an exclamation of sympathy: impotent as he is in the face of evil
and suffering, this is all he can offer.

Va corriendo, andando . . . (p. 125) indicates that the human
condition is flight, that life is a nightmare in which man is
constantly fleeing from evil and suffering. He can never be at
rest, he is always running in terror. The whole poem conveys a
sensation of frantic, headlong flight: it is based on short, broken
lines, enjambment, and on the repetition of the verb *huir* rein-

forced by the neighbouring verbs *ir*, *correr* and *andar*. But flight is futile, for man can never find a refuge from evil, since he carries it about with him, since it is inherent in life and in human nature. Thus the poem offers no possibility of escape: the future will follow the same pattern of misery and suffering as the past and present.

The same nightmarish atmosphere is found in *El acento me pende* . . . (p. 138) where an ominous noise fills the poet with terror. This menacing noise dogs him like an iron ball chained to his foot, varying in pitch and diffusing an air of foreboding. Sensing that something is threatening him, the poet feels that he is too big and too exposed and would like to shrink and disappear from sight. He has a terrible sensation of being judged: the birds perched on the branches of the trees seem to him the incarnation of inhuman judges who are watching over him, waiting for the moment to condemn him. One is reminded of Kafka's *The Trial* where the protagonist is arrested, judged and condemned without even knowing what his crime is. The poet feels himself threatened by some unknown and implacable power of which he fears he will be the victim. Abandoned by other men and feeling that prayer is useless, he finds himself alone in the face of this hostile force. He reacts with pride, affirming that he is strong and does not need help, but his rather forced self-assurance is soon shattered as the noise makes itself heard again. The poem ends with a cry of horror as the poet, alone and defenceless, feels evil bear down upon him.

Los nueve monstruos (p. 134) bears a certain similarity to Camus's *La Peste*. Suffering is seen as a kind of plague which is infesting the universe and the poem is an appeal addressed to mankind announcing a great catastrophe. Suffering is continually spreading and it is spreading at a speed inconceivable to man. The outstanding feature of suffering is its astonishing fertility: suffering begets more suffering. It is a monster which feeds on man, and as it devours him it grows and as it grows its appetite becomes more and more insatiable. The human condition is to suffer an agony that progressively gets worse. In the second stanza the poet affirms that the human condition has never been as critical as it is now and all the resources of civilization are impotent to remedy the situation. Suffering affects everything in the universe: men, animals, inanimate objects. The third stanza projects us into a future which becomes more and more critical as evil spreads, outstripping human progress. It is a flood that contains within it the means of propagating itself. It introduces chaos into life and bears testimony to the presence of some force of evil in the universe. Suffering harasses man from all sides and attacks him in everything he does or touches, and all the things of the earth are condemned to suffer as man does. The poet declares that he cannot put up with this state of affairs any longer and asks what is to be done. The question is addressed to the Minister of Health, but it receives no reply and it is implied that society, with all its political and administrative apparatus, is incapable of remedying the situation. The poem ends with a sigh and a recognition that evil is immense and that it is very difficult for man to overcome it. Yet at the same time the poet invokes his fellow men in solidarity and calls on them to unite and to work together. Thus the poem has positive implications: it suggests that a united humanity, working together in solidarity, might be able to overcome evil and suffering.

The ultimate and most terrible manifestation of the absurd is, of course, death. Perhaps the most poignant lines of the volume are those in which the poet, conscious of the illness that is undermining his body and of the advance of age, senses death to be near. In *Marcha nupcial* (p. 156) he describes himself walking down the aisle to marry death. His train is made up of the acts of his life which flash before his eyes as is said to happen to a drowning man. He experiences a momentary exultation as, like a king reviewing his troops, he recalls the achievements of his life. But exultation immediately gives way to doubt and despair—he has a negative round his neck like a fetter—as he realizes that all the acts of his life have been meaningless. Panic takes possession of him at the speed with which he is being rushed towards death. He is paralysed with terror and stupefaction at the double shock of the realization that all his life has been as nothing and that he is now being pushed into the void. He has reached the frontier that separates life from death and he screams with terror and swallows back tears. He recognizes that his whole being is going to be consumed in death, his animal body in all its insignificance (symbolized by the ant) and his spirit which thirsts after the transcendental (symbolized by the key). Life itself will be consumed. It is a lawsuit which man must inevitably lose and which ends with him being sentenced to death. The cause which the poet is defending is his own existence, his actions and his values, all that he has made of his life. But all these are rendered meaningless by death which effaces from the earth the track he has made and which signals his passage through life. The final stanza seems to suggest that his remains will fertilize the earth from which fresh life will spring. In this sense even man's marriage to death is fertile, since he contributes to the eternal renewal of nature. But this renewal makes a mockery of man and his limitations since he as an individual cannot participate in it.

Vallejo's preoccupation with death is nowhere more clearly expressed than in *Sermón sobre la muerte* (p. 137) where death is seen as an advancing army sweeping before it all the things of life. The poem is based on a series of rhetorical questions revolving around three basic points which particularly torment the poet. Firstly, if man must die, what need does he have of food and sermons? What does it avail him to sustain body and soul if he is to die anyway? All provisions to sustain life are superfluous since they are useless. Secondly, if man must die, why must he die little by little? Why must each moment of life be a death, why must life be a constant and progressive dying? Thirdly, what meaning do human activities and values have in face of death? What lasting significance do the achievements of human civilizations have? Death seems to make life pointless. None the less, the poet expresses his determination to resist death with all the resources he can call forth. He will continue to struggle against the absurd, praying with his whole being for a better world and striving to achieve peace and repose. He will multiply himself so that he is in all places ready to ward off an attack from whatever side it may come. He takes pride in his struggle against the absurd and its ultimate manifestation, death, for it is in this struggle that human dignity resides.

Poemas humanos is dominated by a sense of existential anguish. In *Quiere y no quiere* . . . (p. 127) the poet's bleeding chest is the symbol of the suffering that dominates his life. His attitude towards life is ambivalent. He clings to it, for no matter how horrible it may be, it is preferable to death. But the life of suffering to which he is condemned is intolerable. His anguish springs from the fact that he lives under a constant threat of death, symbolized by the axe raised above his head, and from his inability to realize his deepest longings, symbolized by the bird that cannot fly. Man clings to life, but the poet affirms and reiterates that this is not the kind of life man wishes to lead: he wants more from life than the agony of introspection, the torment of meditating about the absurdity of his situation. Life is cruel: man is born crying, weak and defenceless, and his condition is to suffer. He cannot expect to know why life is like this: all he can do is accept it as it is. But the poet refuses to recognize that there is anything good or splendid about life and affirms that it is a source of anguish.

In *Intensidad y altura* (p. 133) the poet, anguished and embittered, wishes to leave in verse a testimony of his suffering. He wishes to say so many things, but he gets bogged down. Instead of words there emerges only the foam of his anger at the injustice of suffering. He wants to write but he lacks the necessary tranquillity, for he is possessed by the vicious ferocity of a wild beast. He wishes to achieve greatness as an artist, to forge out of his anguish a work of art that will be eternal, but he becomes entangled in obsessive meditations about the miserable and prosaic existence he leads. He runs up against the problem of the inadequacy of language. While the intuition that is the core of a work of art is one and indivisible, language is diverse, is a sum of words which the poet must struggle to organize into a unity. Words tend to be emitted and to become dispersed in the air, and the essential and eternal can be grasped only through great and patient labour. Incapable of finding an adequate expression of his suffering, incapable of writing a testimony that would ennoble his suffering, the poet abandons himself to it. He resigns himself to eating grass, to a way of life that fails to satisfy his deepest appetites. He accepts the diet of suffering that is his portion in life. He even becomes resigned to eating himself, to consuming and destroying himself through obsessive introspection. His only escape is a momentary evasion in the sexual act, in the mechanical repetition of an act that has become stale and humdrum. Ironically he is capable of creation only through the fecundation of the female.

In *Ello es que . . .* (p. 132) the poet describes his home and the life he leads there. His house is nothing but a bare room and it is the image of the emptiness of his life. His life is an unending circle of elementary acts and nothing ever happens to fill it and give it a meaning. In the midst of this emptiness he is a soul living in anguish, engaged in obsessive introspection about his situation and striving to put some order into his life. He laments that his house is nothing but a house, that the happy integrated atmosphere of his childhood home is missing, but he takes some comfort from the fact that it is at least a floor, something solid on which he can find support and to which he can cling. He feels that death is near, that he is now only a skeleton, that his body is stripped of flesh and all the knowledge and culture he has acquired. The objects which surround him become symbols of the death that is threatening him—the spoon is a symbol of the tomb and its inscription is his epitaph—while the cigarettes he smokes one after another point to his anguish. He speaks of his "beloved spoon" and his "dear skeleton": he clings to life for, empty though it may be, it seems desirable in face of death. As death approaches he comes to think of the good things life has to offer and wants to make the most of it. He tries to control himself, to comport himself with dignity so as not to give way to hysterics or to burst into tears, for the anguish that has taken possession of his soul is so overwhelming that the instinct to weep is almost automatic. He

sees himself as a man of 45 whose life has been empty and faced
with a future that holds no prospect but death, and he is powerless
to remedy the situation. He has no alternative but to go on
suffering, participating in the universal mass in which humanity
is the victim, the bread and wine offered up in sacrifice. He
suffers with his whole being, intellectually, emotionally and
physically. He conceives of the possibility of a change in the order
of things: Sunday might become Monday, the various faculties
might change their functions. But he cannot conceive of a change
in the pattern of suffering: he might suffer differently but he
would still suffer. He would still be overwhelmed by a desire to
stifle his anguish, for he is a man and as such his destiny is to
suffer.

Piedra negra sobre una piedra blanca (p. 143) deals with a mood of
spleen. The poem is set in Paris, on a Thursday in autumn, and it
is raining. The poet feels oppressed by the immensity and
impersonalness of the great city; Thursday is for him a day of ill
omen; winter is drawing near; the rain fills him with depression.
The poet feels himself to be impotent, incapable of creating
poetry. He is overcome by listlessness and inertia: he has little
inclination to work and has to force his arm to write. He has a
terrible sense of isolation and feels that everything and everyone
is hostile to him. Such an experience seems to the poet a foretaste
of death: death will simply be a more complete version of the
spleen he is now experiencing and has already experienced on
previous occasions. Hence he can forecast his death and speak of
it as something he has witnessed. Hence he can see himself die,
beaten to death by his fellow men like a child unjustly beaten
for something of which he is innocent. The final lines gather
together the various elements of his suffering in an enumeration:
these are the proof that the world is hostile to him and is beating
him to death.

A feature of *Poemas humanos* is the absence of references to God.
In Vallejo's universe God does not manifest himself: man is
abandoned to his own resources and can expect no aid from a
divine source. *Un pilar soportando consuelos . . .* (p. 125) seems to be

a dramatization of a conflict going on in the poet's mind between his scepticism and his need to believe. Terrified by the thought of death, he is in a church praying. His attention becomes fixed on the two pillars in front of him. They are the external sign of the strength, comfort and support that religion offers in face of death. But the poet cannot manage to pray with his whole being. Part of him remains detached and sceptical, while the other greedily gulps down the hope that religion offers. A series of questions express the poet's inner conflict as he is torn between the reasonings of his intelligence and an irrational hope that prayer might offer a way out of the labyrinth of suffering. He has the momentary illusion that hope is justified, for the pillars seem to be listening to him, but this illusion is immediately destroyed. For the pillars have changed and seem to be simply a projection of the numbness that the poet, weary of kneeling, feels in his legs. The pillars are no longer identified with strength and comfort but are the image of the poet's weariness and loss of hope. He ends the poem by accepting the inevitability of death and abandoning himself to it. He finds consolation not in religion, but in the very completeness of death which annihilates all suffering and liberates him from the terror of dying.

Acaba de pasar . . . (p. 147) recalls Samuel Beckett's *Waiting for Godot*. Vallejo, like Didi and Gogo, is awaiting the arrival of someone who will give a meaning to life. Biblical associations—"el que vendrá", "el que vino en un asno"—suggest a parallel with the coming of Christ: the poet is awaiting a new Messiah who will redeem mankind from the spiritual wilderness in which it is lost. This redeemer will assure man's "triple desarrollo", the reign of harmony and unity, symbolized by the number three. In Beckett's play Godot never comes. Vallejo's imagination gives another twist to this situation: the new Messiah has come and gone but he had nothing to offer that man did not already possess. He has given him only what is stale and worn out. He has done nothing to change the conditions of life nor to enable man to transcend his egoism and his animal nature. He has succeeded only in destroying what remained of the poet's hope and illusions.

Belief in the possibility of another life in which a l man's aspirations would be satisfied has been definitively undermined by him. Far from bringing glad tidings of redemption the Messiah has only increased the poet's anguish. Having nothing to offer, it was as if he had not come at all.

In *Poemas humanos*, as in *Trilce* and *Los heraldos negros*, Vallejo is tormented by the misery of his own situation. However, as we have already noted, he is more and more concerned with the condition of man. For Vallejo man's condition is that of the orphan. Throughout the volume he insists on man's smallness and insignificance. Man is frail and defenceless, ill-equipped to face life: he never ceases to be a child exposed to danger and in need of love and protection. He lives in isolation, completely cut off from his fellow men. His life is utterly empty: he exists in a spiritual vacuum with no transcendental values which would fill his life and give it a meaning; he lives in misery, deprived of the most elementary material comforts. In Vallejo's poetry there are few references to the external scene: the external world of landscapes and buildings does not exist. Vallejian man is alone with his anguish, without a setting to which he can relate his life and which would lend him a support. In *Poemas humanos* man is placed in an extreme situation: he is deprived of all the material and moral barriers that usually protect man against the harshness of life. He finds himself alone and completely naked, face to face with a hostile reality, without defences of any kind.

In *Considerando en frío* . . . (p. 139) Vallejo, in the manner of a prosecuting attorney, analyses the human condition and accumulates evidence proving man's misery and insignificance. He is a fragile, sickly creature who complacently believes himself to be a superior being. He leads an empty, humdrum life, existing from one day to another. He is an animal and such refinements as the combing of the hair only underline his animality. In society he either exploits or is exploited. Time makes a mockery of all that he holds dear. The condition of mankind is hunger, material and spiritual. When he stops to think about his situation, he succumbs to despair, but he does not often think: instead he lives unconsciously and mechanically, finding diversion in work and other activities. Man awakens contradictory emotions in the poet: love and solidarity; hatred and scorn, mingled with love; the indifference that one feels for an insect. Yet having coldly proved man's insignificance, Vallejo is overcome by tenderness and, calling the human animal over to him, embraces him fraternally. He feels an instinctive solidarity with man that proves stronger than his reason.

El alma que sufrió de ser su cuerpo (p. 145) presents the poet as a doctor coldly diagnosing the illness of a patient (at once man and the poet himself) and ruthlessly revealing to him the seriousness of his condition. Throughout the poem Vallejo insists that man is a poor insignificant creature and that his destiny is to suffer. He also suggests some of the causes of his suffering. Man's anguish springs partly from his tendency to think about life which reveals to him the absurdity of existence. It springs partly from the conflict between his animal nature and the spiritual and the domination of the latter by the former. It proceeds in part from the period of crisis in which modern man lives, from the collapse of traditional values and beliefs. He also suggests that it proceeds from the conditions of life itself, that suffering is something inherent in existence. The poem ends with a discussion between the poet and man. The latter refuses to accept the poet's diagnosis, refuses to recognize that he is simply an insignificant animal. Then the poet takes pity on him and offers him his hand, but in so doing he makes a slip of the tongue and asks for his paw. This humour is in reality a reiteration of the whole poem. Throughout the poet has attempted to make man recognize his condition, but his diagnosis has been rejected, so he abandons his arguments and tries to reduce man by irony, treating him as an animal. The poet, then, diagnoses man's illness, but he does not prescribe a remedy. Instead he ends the poem by telling man to live out his destiny of suffering: man's illness appears to be incurable.

For Vallejo the absurdity and chaos of the universe is reflected in a society divided by the conflict of classes. Society—or, more exactly, capitalist society—is a jungle in which the strong and powerful exploit and oppress the weak and the humble, "la dictudura de unos cuantos explotadores sobre la masa de productores".[1] In *Poemas humanos* a series of poems portray the miserable condition of the underprivileged. Thus *La rueda del hambriento* (p. 130) is the delirious monologue of a starving man as he contemplates his misery. His internal body is being expelled through his mouth and he is engaged in the act of excretion. These acts are the opposite of eating: not only does he have nothing to eat but he feels as if his own being were being taken from him. It is as if misery had caught him on the end of a stick and pulled him out of his body like a mussel out of its shell. From the depths of his misery he directs an appeal to some unknown and unheeding onlooker—the reader, society, humanity, God. His appeal has the tone of a prayer, in parts its formula is that of the *Pater Noster*, and it recalls a passage from St. Matthew's Gospel (vii. 8–11). He appeals for the humblest thing on earth, a stone, on which to rest, any stone, the stone which is of no use to anyone else or which is used as an instrument of injustice. He appeals for bread to mitigate his hunger. He receives no reply and in the latter part of the poem the appeal becomes quicker and more insistent. He fears that he is being misunderstood and his final appeal, "en español", becomes more explicit and more frenzied. Then it tapers off in a promise to go away. He realizes that he is being importunate, that he is making the listener feel uncomfortable, and he himself feels humiliated and ashamed. But his pleas come up against a wall of silence, and, all his strength and hope exhausted, he returns to the contemplation of his misery. The poem ends, as it began, with an exclamation of suffering: the starving man is unable to break out of the vicious circle of his misery and receives no help from anyone.

París, octubre 1936 (p. 136) introduces us to one of society's pariahs, the poor tramp whose only refuge is the park bench and who has no place in the life of the great city. By means of a play on words he ironically refers to his situation as that of a banker with an important position and shares. He resolves to move off

---

[1] César Vallejo, *Rusia en 1931*, Lima, 1965, p. 139.

and to leave his misery behind him. However, it soon becomes clear that the way in which he proposes to escape from his misery is through death. He has lost the will to go on living and has anticipated death by yielding himself up to it. Yet paradoxically his parting is also a birth, for through death he will achieve liberation. He describes himself as someone already dead, the mere appearance of a human being, a zombie casting off shadows and moving unnoticed among the living. He still goes through the motions of living and his bodily form and his clothing are there as an alibi proving that he exists, but he is already dead since he has renounced life and is only waiting for death to carry him off.

Los desgraciados (p. 150) is set in a cheap hotel room where one of society's unfortunates is lying in bed trying to shut out of his mind the thought of having to go through another day of misery. Throughout the poem the poet announces to him the approach of the new day: by his insistence he wishes to draw the *desgraciado* from his disheartenment and to get him to face up to his situation with dignity and courage. He urges him to make an effort of will and to rise and dress and go out and face the new day. He urges him to endure the pangs of hunger, the pains of his organs tormented by lack of food, and to reflect on his situation and seek a way out of it instead of succumbing to defeatist and self-pitying meditations. He must not give way to lamentation, for lamentation is a luxury the poor cannot afford. His situation is so desperate that he must react and pull himself together. He must put his trust in the future and hope for the white thread of good fortune. He must review the different links of the chain of his suffering and put self-pity behind him. He must put on his soul, assuming the will to live and infusing life into his inert body. The hotel has begun to come to life and the noise of people moving about awakened the *desgraciado*, opening his eyes to a world of horror. He trembles, his head dizzy with hunger and the claims of his stomach uppermost in his mind. Meanwhile the other unfortunates who live in the same hotel are still sleeping peacefully, freed from their universe of misery. As the *desgraciado* reflects that it is only in sleep that the poor can find peace, resentment oozes out of all the pores of his body at the injustice of the misery he has to endure. Since the other *desgraciados* are asleep, he feels himself completely alone in his misery, even though he knows that the others are in the same situation as he is. The poet urges him to anaesthetize himself against suffering as in sleep. He must intensify his efforts to struggle against his misery, going out to fight his hunger and thirst on all sides. In the last stanza day is now breaking and poet reiterates that the *desgraciado* must overcome his fear and intensify his will to live. For the only way in which he can break out of his misery is by facing up to it. The poet points out to the *desgraciado* how desperate his situation is. All his misery is to be seen in his crutch, in his worn and used trousers. He lives in a world where injustice is permanent. He dreamed that he achieved the miracle of living on nothing, but in fact he is defeated and crushed by everything. The poem opens on to an indefinite future of misery unless something is done to remedy the situation.

Parado en una piedra . . . (p. 152) was inspired by the spectacle of the mass unemployment that hit the Western world during the Depression. The poem concentrates on the figure of one of the unemployed, an outcast on the margin of bourgeois society. Hunger causes his stomach to rumble. Fleas cling to his body. His only possessions are a few insignificant articles whose worthlessness accentuates his destitution. This is the drama of the worker who has been excluded and reduced to uselessness. This is a man who sweated in work but who now sweats inwards. Now that his energies are unused they are secreted and rot within him. With all his capacity to create, to build a better world, with all his mastery of technique and matter, he is reduced to inactivity, a phenomenon which is repeated millions of times. All his potentialities, crying out to be used, are wasted, and Vallejo's impassioned reiteration raises this terrible waste to the level of a cosmic catastrophe. Work is seen as a law of nature and an integral part of the creative forces of the universe. The disruption of that law involves a disruption of the whole of nature. Nature stops in solidarity and the earth itself comes to a halt stupefied by this absurd situation. With all his capacity to produce wealth, he lacks the means to feed himself, while the non-productive elements of society live in luxury and ease. In face of such injustice he is filled with blind rage, and his whole being, his hunger, his misery, the few miserable possessions that are the symbol of his destitution, cry out in protest.

The spectacle of suffering moves the poet to love and he identifies himself with the underdogs of bourgeois society. This does not mean, however, that he attributes all suffering to an evil social system or that he believes suffering to be limited to any section of humanity. The victims of society are also men crushed by life and the poet's love embraces the whole of suffering humanity. Thus, *Traspié entre dos estrellas* (p. 140) is an act of love in which Vallejo feels the suffering of all the unfortunates of the earth as his own and bestows his love on them in a manner recalling the Beatitudes. He expresses his love of man plunged in an obscure everyday misery, the misery of the abandoned animal whose life never rises above the earth, above his physical condition and above an elemental existence. This is a love that embraces everyone in the universe, rich as well as poor, criminal as well as honest man, for everyone in the universe suffers. But it is a love that is powerless to improve the lot of those who suffer and which has to limit itself to exclamations of tenderness.

In *Me viene, hay días* ... (p. 149) Vallejo's love of man is seen as an emotion so strong that it demands to express itself. He wants to love all men whether they want his love or not and he wants to put his love into action. Like Christ, he wishes to give himself to the sick, the poor and the humble, and like Christ, he wishes to make the good and the respectable understand the criminal. He insists on the universality of his love: it is "interhuman" and it is parochial in that he sees the world as one large community and all men as his neighbours. This is a love that embraces all men— the poor, the weak, the evil, even his enemies. It is a love that ignores the barriers of morality. He even wishes to help the murderer to kill, an idea that appals his conscience but which indicates that his love extends even to those who are generally considered unworthy of love. He concludes the poem by wishing that he, a suffering creature like his fellow men, might live happily instead of torturing and tormenting himself with thoughts of the absurdity of existence.

Vallejo, then, identifies existence with pain and suffering. In *Poemas humanos* suffering takes on a multiplicity of forms. Few poets have insisted as Vallejo does on the horrors of physical suffering: poverty, hunger, illness. But it must be emphasized that physical suffering is always accompanied by an existential anguish: a sense of the meaninglessness of existence, of weariness and defeat; a consciousness of the passing of time; a terror of death.

Vallejo comes to conceive of a whole universe united in suffering. In *Voy a hablar de la esperanza* (p. 159) he affirms that he does not suffer personally: his individual suffering is simply part of the cosmic suffering. He does not suffer as César Vallejo or as a poet, for his suffering has nothing to do with his own particular situation. His suffering cannot be explained in terms of some personal misfortune, for it lacks a specific cause and everything is its cause. His is the suffering of a whole universe united in pain. In this poem Vallejo loses consciousness of his personal identity and his individual suffering as he feels himself participate in the universal suffering. Yet paradoxically this poem opens the door to hope, as the title indicates. For Vallejo man's salvation lies in human solidarity, and there exists the possibility of salvation from the moment that men become united, from the moment that the individual loses his individual consciousness and identifies himself with his fellows, even if it is only through suffering.

Poemas humanos, then, portrays the absurdity of the world as it is at present. Yet many of the poems we have seen contain positive implications. Thus, if in *El alma que sufrió de ser su cuerpo* (p. 145) Vallejo tries to force man to recognize the seriousness of his condition, it is in the hope that this will be the first step towards remedying it. Similarly in *Oye a tu masa . . .* (p. 155) Vallejo calls on man to consider his crisis in order to find a way out of it. Instead of succumbing to self-pity he must face up to his situation. He must take account of his duality, of the conflicting forces within him: the inert mass of his body and the spirit that strives to reach the heights; the social personality of the civilized man that forces his natural impulses to lie dormant and the impulses of the natural man that take over in sleep when the consciousness is no longer in control. He must recognize that life is a precarious ride on a horrible beast. He must see himself as a fragile creature destined to die. He must analyse and get to know himself in a systematic fashion, and at the same time he must attempt to reconstruct and reshape his life. He must oppose to evil and death all the weapons of which the human mind is capable, but without presuming to be master of the universe, recognizing the presence of death and the absurd which are constantly undermining life. He must think about his situation, but without succumbing to obsessive introspection. In that way he may find a solution.

Other poems, such as *Los nueve monstruos* (p. 134) and *Voy a hablar de la esperanza* (p. 159), suggest that if there is a way out of the impasse of the absurd it is through human solidarity. The same notion is expressed in *Hasta el día en que vuelva* . . . (p. 134). Here life is seen as a journey which ends at its starting-point: the poet must live his life knowing that he must return to the void from which he has come, symbolized by the stone. He goes through life a cripple, incomplete and incapable of attaining his goals, embittered by one disappointment after another, yet holding his head erect. The poet affirms that the absurdity of existence does not give man the right to comport himself in a cynical and egoistic fashion: he has a responsibility towards his fellow men. He sees death as a day of final judgement but significantly speaks not of a judge but of judges: he will be judged not by God but by his fellow men and the criterion of a good life is his comportment towards others. The poem ends with an apotheosis of man: in spite of the fact that he must disappear into the void, in spite of the absurdity of life and his own insignificance, man can achieve a certain grandeur. The context of the poem seems to imply that he will do so by facing up to the misery of life with dignity and by recognizing and fulfilling his responsibility towards his fellows.

For Vallejo the way out of the impasse of human misery is through the Communist Revolution. Communism offers the possibility of a transformation of the conditions of life. Thus he quotes Marx: "Los filósofos, — dice Marx, — no han hecho hasta ahora sino interpretar el mundo de diversas maneras. De lo que se trata es de transformarlo."[1] This transformation will be brought about by producing a revolution in men's souls: "La Revolución no significa la caída del Zar ni la toma del poder por los obreros. Es lo que hoy ocurre en el corazón de las familias y de las gentes. Esto es la Revolución."[2] Through Communism the individual mentality of capitalist society will give way to a new collective mentality. Men will acquire a spirit of brotherly love and human solidarity and will subordinate their private interests to the interests of their fellow men. They will learn to work together as brothers in the common good. Science and technology will be placed at the service of man instead of serving the interests of a privileged group. It is significant that much of Vallejo's later poetry should exalt the manual worker: he is the productive element of society, he has an instinctive sense of solidarity, and his labour will be the foundation of a new world.

For Vallejo the Revolution holds out the possibility of Redemption, and it will be carried out in two stages. Firstly, the Revolution will eliminate social injustice and create a just and egalitarian society. Then Vallejo dreams of a new universal society, without frontiers, in which all men will be united in love and will work together to eliminate evil and to create a unified and harmonious world. In this way man will cease to be the prisoner of his individual consciousness, he will overcome his present anguish, and life will acquire a meaning and a direction. Vallejo believes, too, that when all mankind is united in love, when all men work together as brothers, when science and technology are placed at

[1] C. Vallejo, 'El pensamiento revolucionario', *Mundial*, Lima, 3 May 1929.
[2] 'Una tragedia inédita de Vallejo', *Letras Peruanas*, 7, 1952, p. 108.

the service of humanity, then man will be capable of everything: he will dominate nature and control his destiny.

Hence in several poems in *Poemas humanos* and in *España . . .* Vallejo is speaking on two complementary levels. On the one hand, he is a revolutionary proclaiming the liberation of the oppressed through the proletarian revolution. But at the same time he is a prophet foretelling the total redemption of man: drawing inspiration from the Bible and employing a religious terminology, he sings of the paradise that will be conquered on earth by a united humanity. In the new universal society which Vallejo foresees not only will the social structure be rectified but the conditions of life will be transformed; not only will injustice be eliminated but evil will be abolished; not only will man be freed from oppression but he will overcome the absurd and attain a full and harmonious life. It is essential, however, to understand that Vallejo is not thinking of a sudden miracle worked by brotherly love. He is thinking of a distant future in which the world will have been transformed by science and technology employed by a united humanity in the service of man: "El socialismo suprimirá también el frío. Lo suprimirá con los progresos de la industria. Las posibilidades de la ciencia y de la técnica son infinitas."[1]

The poems of *España . . .* refer to the Spanish Civil War and celebrate the heroes of the Republic. But for Vallejo this is not simply a struggle of the workers against Fascism: it is an episode of man's struggle to create the new universal society and the Republic is the symbol of that society. Thus in the *Himno a los voluntarios de la República*[2] (p. 161) Vallejo prophesies the reign of peace, harmony and justice that will come into being as a result of the sacrifice of the Republican militiamen. This part of the poem (ll. 90–113) is modelled on the prophecies of Isaiah (xi. 6–8; xxv. 8; xxix. 18; xxxv. 5–6). In this new world, all men will love. Man's physical needs will be satisfied: all men will be able to eat the food that was denied to the *voluntarios*. This world will be a haven where humanity will be able to rest at the end of its

---

[1] C. Vallejo, *Rusia ante el segundo plan quinquenal*, Lima, 1965, p. 130.
[2] Henceforth this poem will be referred to as the *Himno*.

long pilgrimage. Man will achieve a new unity: the human animal who instinctively follows the impulses of his body and the thinker who descends into the depths of his soul will fuse together in the one person. Not only will the social structure be corrected but nature itself will be dominated. The dumb and the lame will embrace one another in joy at having been freed from their defects. Having completed the journey of darkness and suffering, the blind will begin the return journey of joy and light. The deaf will palpitate with emotion, intoxicated by the revelation of sound. Man will arrive at true wisdom, the ignorant ascending towards knowledge and the wise descending from the heights of abstract thought. The forces of life will triumph over the absurd and death. All the species will be united in fraternal love and a solidarity will be established between the most disparate elements. The imperfections of nature will be overcome: the deformed will be reborn perfectly formed. All social distinctions will disappear and the greatest plagues facing man will be overcome: all men will work, there will be no unemployed and no idle rich; all men will be fertile and productive; all men will be intelligent and understanding.

The culmination of all Vallejo's work is *Masa* (p. 164). This poem is based on the resurrection of Lazarus (John xi. 43–44) and is a prophetic vision of man's victory over the absurd. The poem is concentrated on the corpse of a Republican soldier lying on the battlefield. One of his companions comes up to him and tries to revive him by reminding him of the love he has for him. Two men approach, then a group which rises to 500 thousand, then millions of individuals. They all beg him to go on living, but the corpse remains dead. The emotional progression is resolved in the final stanza where the miracle of the resurrection takes place. All the men of the earth surround the corpse and when the latter sees all men united he comes back to life. The implication of the poem is that the love of an individual or of many individuals is powerless in face of evil. But when all men adopt the values of the *voluntario*, when all men come together in brotherly love, when every member of the human race is part of a universal society ruled by love, then man will be capable of conquering evil. The resurrection of the dead soldier symbolizes man's eventual domination of nature and destiny.

It is clear that Vallejo's is a highly personal brand of Communism. It is to be remembered that Vallejo always had an instinctive sense of solidarity with his fellow men and that love was always one of his great ideals. His dream of a universal society ruled by love was shaped partly by his Christian upbringing. While Vallejo is not a Christian, he always conserved the Christian ideal of brotherly love. It is significant that he should see the ideal world of the future in mainly biblical terms and that his proletarian heroes should appear as new Christs. It is to be emphasized, however, that the kingdom of heaven which Vallejo prophesies will be achieved on earth and that the redeemer will not be God made man but man himself. In a sense, too, his ideal of a universal society ruled by love is simply a projection on to a universal plane of Vallejo's private ideal of the home and the family: the new society will be the home of everyone and all of humanity will be a single family. It is significant that he should refer to Russian society as "el hogar de los hogares".[1] Significantly, too, the Spanish Republic is described as "la madre España": the new society is a universal mother offering love and protection to all the children of the earth.

Despite the messianic nature of his later poetry Vallejo realizes that theories and doctrines in themselves are insufficient to change the world. He realizes that men must have recourse to practical action, that they must take up arms and fight. Thus in the *Himno* (ll. 138–67) (p. 165) he calls on the *voluntarios* to kill in order to create a new and better life. They must kill the forces of death. The enemy who is killing Republican soldiers is only part of a wider enemy: all those who oppress the weak and defenceless. They are fighting against those who oppress children, mothers, old men, even dogs. They are fighting in the same cause as the beggar who joyfully embraces his misery as a means of awakening men's consciences, the nurse who weeps at the sight

[1] *Rusia en 1931*, p. 209.

of suffering as she strives to alleviate it, the priest on his knees praying for suffering humanity. Vallejo urges the *voluntarios* to kill in order to bring about a life where there will be no death, to kill those with evil in their hearts to make way for a new humanity which will love. He urges them to kill in order to bring about a world where all men will be free, even their enemies, and where there will be peace without suffering. They must kill in order to bring about the kingdom of Christ in which the humble will be exalted. Vallejo, then, believes in the necessity of armed revolution, but it is to be emphasized once again that for him the Revolution is not simply a struggle of the workers against capitalism: it is a struggle of humanity to create a world of peace and love.

Like Milton, Vallejo also believes that "They also serve who only stand and wait". He has an attitude towards suffering similar to that of the Christians: the acceptance of misery can be a positive factor. The destitute, the weak and the defenceless can play their part in man's redemption by accepting their misery with dignity—but not with resignation: here Vallejo differs from the Christian. Their misery awakens in men's consciences a recognition of the need for justice, and inspires in men's hearts love and compassion. Since these are the forces that Vallejo believes will bring about redemption, misery can become an instrument of redemption and the suffering in a sense can become redeemers.

In *Los desgraciados* (p. 150) we have seen Vallejo urge the *desgraciado* to face up to his misery. In the latter part of the poem he urges him not to seek to alleviate his situation by begging for charity from the rich. Charity is a palliative in an unjust society, it serves only to ease the conscience of the rich, and helps preserve injustice. The *desgraciado* must accept his misery uncompromisingly. He must poke his cold, he must feed his misery in the sense of standing firm in his position and intransigently rejecting charity. The sight of the *desgraciado*'s misery warms the poet, inspiring him with love and leading him to identify himself with him in his condition as victim of society. But if he can awaken these sentiments in the poet he can awaken them in others and thus prepare the way for man's redemption. In this way he can become a victim in another sense, a victim like Christ whose sacrifice will lead to redemption. Hence the poet urges him to put on his body, to accept his misery. In the sixth stanza the *leitmotiv* "Ya va a venir el día" acquires a double sense: the poet is announcing not merely the dawn of another day of misery but also the approach of the day of redemption. The *desgraciado*'s weariness and misery will be followed by rejoicing. There will be a new cosmic unity in which all the elements will be in harmony. The whole universe will celebrate with flags the death of the old world and the birth of the new. As a result of the *desgraciado*'s proud and uncompromising acceptance of his misery, the strong and the powerful will walk in company with the weak and the humble as prophesied by Isaiah (xi. 6). Even businessmen, those who have the means of satisfying his hunger, will think of helping the poor and the hungry. This time will come, but the present is the moment of sacrifice. During this sacrifice—seen as a mass, a sacrifice like Christ's—he cannot count on help from anyone, for he must face it alone, without friends. He must embrace his sacrifice dressing himself in the sun, with hope for the future.

Los mendigos . . . (p. 166) deals with a similar theme. For Vallejo the war in Spain is part of a wider war which humanity is waging against evil and injustice. The Spanish Front is thus a symbol of the universal front in which the poor and the destitute cry out and struggle for justice. It is in this sense that Vallejo sees all the beggars of the world united in the cause of Spain. The beggars raise their misery into an instrument of redemption since it awakens consciences and inspires love. The beggars stretching out their hands in all the capitals of the world are like the Apostles who travelled the roads of the earth on foot to evangelize it. Thus, in its way, the non-violent struggle of the defenceless is just as effective as the military action of the soldiers of the Republic. Suffering unleashes a moral revolution and thus kills without arms. Misery and suffering are thus non-violent weapons in the struggle to conquer the kingdom of peace, justice and happiness.

Vallejo seems to have believed that humanity was on the eve of a new epoch, that his ideals were beginning to become a reality. In *Al revés de las aves* . . . (p. 143) he sings as a reality a world in which peace, harmony and unity reign among men. This is a world in which the law of the jungle, symbolized by birds of prey, has been superseded. Virtue and vice, good and evil, honesty and perfidy, symbolized by *el Sincero* and his grandchildren, have come together. In this poem the techniques of oxymoron and paradox translate a new cosmic unity in which all opposites have been reconciled and all contradictions resolved. Men overcome their differences and come together. Greatness is born of humility. The horror of life has given way to peace and well-being. Vallejo tends to see life as a savage beast which man cannot control but here the monster that is life has become docile: this is a world in which man dominates and controls his destiny. The workers, freed from oppression and injustice, sing with happiness and the poet participates in the general rejoicing. Later in a parenthesis Vallejo makes a commentary which clarifies the sense of the poem. The composition is an allegory of the world political situation; the poet is speaking of the revolutionary movement that swept the world and seemed to be triumphing; he is referring to the twenties and thirties in which it really seemed that man was entering a new era.

Vallejo saw the new society in the process of being born in Russia and in Spain. *Rusia en 1931* reveals that he believed that his ideals were in the process of being realized in the Soviet Union. In the *Himno* (ll. 22–31) (p. 161) he sings the victory of the Popular Front in the elections of February 1936 as the dawn of a new era. In Spain the Revolution was pacific. This was a day that was at last a day, a day bathed in light and not simply another day of darkness. In this election the Spanish people put an end to the oppression into which it had been born. The despots were already in fetters and even their bacterias of corruption and vice were enchained.

At the same time Vallejo sees a new kind of man emerge. This is a man who is characterized by a spirit of universal love, who dedicates his life to the service of his fellow men, who sacrifices himself to create a better world for mankind. In Vallejo's poetry this new man is embodied in the worker who takes up arms to carry out the Revolution. His two great prototypes are the Russian Bolshevist and the Spanish *miliciano*. Vallejo establishes a comparison between these men and Christ: these are the men who will redeem mankind.

Salutación angélica (p. 128) makes an implicit comparison between the Bolshevist and Christ. The poem is based on a passage from St. Luke's Gospel (i. 26–36) in which the Angel Gabriel greets Mary and announces that she has been chosen from all the women of the earth to give birth to the Redeemer. Vallejo greets the Bolshevist and announces to him that he has been elected from all the men of the earth—presumably to redeem mankind. What distinguishes the Bolshevist from other men is his spirit of brotherly love, of human solidarity. All his acts proceed from his breast, are the fruit of love. In a sense he is a man like others: he is a family man, a father, a husband, a loved one. The difference lies in that he raises family love to a universal value: he no longer thinks in terms of his own family but of the human family. And not only does he feel love towards all men but he shows it and puts it into practice: his love is seen in his gestures, his face, his legs, his whole being. His love embraces all the men of the earth and knows no frontiers, and in this sense his smile, the expression of his love, is a blank passport. The Bolshevist is characterized by his activity: while other men are concerned only with comfort and tranquillity, his life is dedicated to work in the service of humanity. In the course of a life in which he is in constant danger of death, he takes up arms and kills to conquer a better world. He kills out of love, in an embrace that envelops all men, with a love that is healthy in that it creates new life. The Bolshevist's devotion to his cause is passionate, but his passion has a solid foundation, is based on a rationally thought-out doctrine. He walks with firm steps, for his are the steps of a new man, of a humanity advancing towards a new life. The poet longs to be like the Bolshevist, but he is aware of a great gulf separating them. He is conscious of his own weakness; he feels himself to be unworthy, to be lacking the constancy and dedication of the Bolshevist; he feels himself guilty of egoism and vanity. The Bolshevist's superiority pains him because it makes him feel insignificant by comparison. In this poem Vallejo is conscious of his own limitations and imperfections which prevent him from following the example of the Bolshevist. He is still the old man, the Bolshevist is the new.

In the *Himno* (p. 161) Vallejo raises his voice to exalt the *miliciano*, the second great prototype of the new man. The *miliciano* is not simply a soldier fulfilling his duty: he is a volunteer who kills and embraces death in the cause of humanity. It is his heart that marches to the front: he fights for love. Like Christ, he suffers an "agonía mundial" (see Mark xiv. 32), he suffers for all mankind. This is a new Christ intrepidly marching to embrace his Cross to redeem mankind, to create a new world. In his presence the poet does not know what to do nor where to put himself. He is overwhelmed by humility and gratitude. He humbly removes his hat in respect. This is an impersonal gesture, the gesture of the poet as representative of all humanity which owes gratitude to the *voluntario*. The *miliciano* is the architect of a new world, a Christ whose falls will redeem mankind. He is a superior being who brings honour to the human species, who gives a new dignity to the human animal. However, the poet is conscious of an enormous gulf between him and the new redeemer. He is conscious of his own inferiority, of his inability to imitate the *miliciano*'s example. He feels himself to be an animal at the dawn of evolution, a prisoner of his own individuality. The grandeur of the *miliciano* will not fit into his miserable and insignificant body. Only his appearance is great: in reality he is a small, fragile thing that breaks in contact with the superior attitudes and activity of the *miliciano*. Hence, he asks to be left alone, as he is. As Paoli has observed,[1] Vallejo's attitude here is that of the saint or mystic who despairs at his own imperfection and his inability to live in God's image.

[1] Roberto Paoli, *Poesie, di César Vallejo*, Milan, 1964, p. ccviii. My interpretation of this poem owes much to Dr. Paoli.

Later (ll. 32–39) Vallejo describes the struggle of the *milicianos* as passions rather than battles. They are passions in that they are driven by an irrepressible enthusiasm to create a new world, but also in that they are a sacrifice, like Christ's, which will bring redemption. Their action is born of suffering, of the suffering of the masses who hope to acquire the right to be men. This is not a war like other wars and death in this war is not like other deaths: it is a war whose end is peace among men, it is a death that will redeem mankind. Like Christ, the *miliciano* raises himself to the first power of martyrdom.

The *miliciano*'s body is offered up in sacrifice (ll. 56–62), but by falling in death he raises himself up, for he transcends death in the cause he leaves behind him, in the flame of the ideal that lives on. His sacrifice inspires the weak and the unfortunate, opens the eyes of the enemy to the values of the new society of which Spain is the symbol, and calls forth strength, fortitude and action from the pacific.

The *miliciano* is a proletarian dying for the whole universe, out of love for the whole of humanity, even his enemy. All his activity is directed towards a harmony in which the conflict between man's grandeur and misery will be resolved. It is towards this end that his violence, spontaneous yet methodical, is directed. He is a liberator converting instruments of oppression into instruments of liberty. But for his efforts the infinite and eternal would remain inaccessible, man would still be incomplete like a headless nail, the world would still be plunged in darkness, pity would still be lacking in the world and even the corpses would remain unburied. Significantly, the new redeemer is a manual worker. It is the workers with their labour and sense of common cause who will build the new society. To bring it about they take up arms and become warriors. Because of their sacrifice in accepting death light and abundance will be born in the world, everything will be converted into gold, and gold will be truly gold, untainted by imperfection. Thanks to them a new golden age will come into being.

Later Vallejo establishes an even more explicit parallel between the *miliciano* and Christ with a prayer based on the *Pater noster*. Significantly he substitutes the Marxist term "brother" for the Christian term "Father". This is the prayer of the poet as representative of all guilty humanity: if humanity recognizes in the *miliciano* a victim sacrificed for its sins, if it recognizes that outside the values he incarnates there can be no redemption, if it adopts the *miliciano*'s values and seeks to follow his example, then humanity can become worthy and capable of redemption. Vallejo then goes on to evoke the volunteers who have come from all the corners of the earth to fight for the cause of the Republic. The column of combatants sings a song of death which para-doxically is a song of the dawn, since the death towards which they are marching will open up a new world. These volunteers are not the unknown soldiers of ordinary wars, the cannon fodder designated by numbers; they have a name, not an indi-vidual name but a name that is universal, that links them with all the men of the earth, a name that resounds in an embrace: brother. These volunteers who carry within them the climate of their region, heroes from every part of the globe, are at once victims and victors: as individuals they are victims, but as a mass they are triumphant. Thus it becomes clear in what sense the *miliciano* and the Bolshevist are redeemers: by their life and exam-ple they spread the values that will redeem man and by their death they contribute to the victory of the revolutionary cause. Redemption will come with the eventual triumph of the cause.

Vallejo, then, seems to have believed that humanity was on the eve of a new era, but he soon realized that his hopes were to be frustrated. In *Al revés de las aves* . . . (p. 143) the harmony and unity that the poet had celebrated in the early stanzas dissolves in the latter part of the poem. The various characters who, filled with hope and illusion, had come together and embraced, now go their separate ways, disheartened and in despair. The poet perceives that man has been unable to overcome evil, the evil that pursues him and causes him to suffer, the evil that he carries within him and makes him a vicious animal. Since the poem is an allegory of the political situation, it is evident that the poet's disillusionment springs from the frustration of the Revolution.

The poem seems to allude to the imminent fall of the Spanish Republic, though possibly it also refers to other countries. Vallejo saw with sadness and rage that the world revolution would not be achieved in his lifetime.

In the poem *España, aparta de mí este cáliz* (p. 168) Vallejo has a premonition of the fall of the Spanish Republic. The title recalls the words of Christ in the Garden of Gethsemane (Matthew xxvi. 39) and tells us that Vallejo wants to be excused this last chalice of suffering. To drive the thought of defeat out of his mind he tries to convince himself that it is an absurd hypothesis. None the less he knows in his heart that defeat is close at hand. In his last book there reappears one of the main themes of his early works: orphanhood. Spain, the symbol of the new society, of the universal family, is a mother who protects all the children of the earth. If the Republic falls, if the universal Mother dies, then all the children of the earth will be orphaned. They will no longer have a normal development and they will even undergo a regression, falling into ignorance and suffering. However, the poet advises them that if the Mother leaves them orphaned, they must not succumb to despair: they must react, they must go out and look for the Mother. Even if the Revolution fails in Spain and the new society is frustrated, man must continue struggling to make them become a reality. Even if evil and the absurd prevail, man must continue struggling to realize his dreams of a harmonious and unified world. This is the final note of Vallejo's poetry. It is significant that the poems of *España* . . . were written in the knowledge that the Republic would be crushed and yet celebrate the triumph of the revolutionary cause: Vallejo sees beyond immediate failures and disappointments to the eventual triumph of the Revolution and the redemption of man.

Though obscurities still exist, *Poemas humanos* is less difficult, less incoherent, more immediately communicative than *Trilce*. In a sense it represents a break with *Trilce*, a reaction away from the avant-garde mentality towards a poetry more easily accessible to the ordinary reader. It is also an evolution. In *Trilce* the

desire to innovate tended to carry the poet to extremes of inco-
herence and hermeticism. Now he has mastered the new tech-
niques and they no longer obtrude but exist alongside more
traditional techniques. In a sense *Poemas humanos* might be said
to be more "classical".

The poems are less concentrated than in *Trilce*, though density
and intensity are still the outstanding features. On the whole the
poems are longer and the poet's inspiration more sustained: the
emotion seems to flow out of the poet like a river in flood. This,
of course, does not mean that the poems are disorganized: the
poet controls and directs the poetic emotion. Indeed, a character-
istic of the book is the return to more traditional forms in some
of the shorter poems: *Intensidad y altura* (p. 133), *Piedra negra
sobre una piedra blanca* (p. 143) and *Marcha nupcial* (p. 156) are
regular, or almost regular, sonnets. Other poems are characterized
by their utter simplicity of form. Thus, *Un hombre pasa . . .* (p. 146)
and *¿ Qué me da . . . ?* (p. 154) consist of series of couplets.

Most of the poems have the form of a monologue or of a
dialogue with someone who does not answer. At times, as in *El
alma que sufrió de ser su cuerpo* (p. 145), it is difficult to know
whether this silent interlocutor is man or the poet's other self:
usually it is both at the same time. The poems register the poet's
meditations on life. They abound in syntactic elements—*puesto
que, sin embargo, así, tal, pues, en suma*, etc.—which give them some-
thing of the tone of a rational discourse. But their movement,
far from being logical, follows the twistings and turnings of a
tormented mind. Many poems do not begin in the strict sense of
the word but rather introduce us into the course of an obsessive
meditation that has begun much earlier. Such poems usually open
with some conjunctive expression that links the composition to
the previous meditation: "Ello es que . . ." (p. 132); "Y, en fin,
pasando luego al dominio de la muerte" (p. 137). Equally the
poems seldom reach a conclusion: they lead nowhere, for the
poet is unable to find a way out of the vicious circle of his obses-
sions. In some cases the poem does a complete circle and comes
back to its starting-point in the final lines: *El acento me pende . . .*

(p. 138), *Traspié entre dos estrellas* (p. 140). In others the last stanza gathers together the various threads of the poem in an enumeration: *Los nueve monstruos* (p. 134), *Piedra negra sobre una piedra blanca* (p. 143). In others such as *El alma que sufrió de ser su cuerpo* (p. 145) and *¡ Y si después de tantas palabras . . . !* (p. 155) the poet resorts to some humorous device to bring the poem to a close. Many poems, then, do not begin or end: in a sense *Poemas humanos* is one great obsessive meditation on human suffering of which each poem is only a moment.

Other poems do not have the form of a monologue but are allegories or parables of the human situation: *Existe un mutilado . . .* (p. 157), *Al revés de las aves . . .* (p. 143), *Nómina de huesos* (p. 157), *Masa* (p. 167). Others are hymns in that in them the poet's voice is raised in exaltation. Most of the poems of *España . . .* fall into this category, but it also embraces poems such as *Salutación angélica* (p. 128).

Poemas humanos is characterized by a grave religious tone, which is achieved partly by the use of the hendecasyllable as the predominant line in the book. As we have seen, some poems could be described as parables or hymns. At times Vallejo insistently repeats formulae in the manner of a litany: "Y el mueble tuvo en su cajón, dolor, / el corazón, en su cajón, dolor, / la lagartija, en su cajón, dolor" (p. 135). A number of poems bear religious titles: *Epístola a los transeúntes* (p. 126), *Sermón sobre la muerte* (p. 137). Biblical associations and religious symbolism abound. Thus *Traspié entre dos estrellas* (p. 140) echoes the Beatitudes. *La rueda del hambriento* (p. 130) has the tone of a prayer, its formula is that of the *Pater noster*, and it contains allusions to the Gospel of Saint Matthew (iv. 3; vii. 7–11; viii. 20). This religious tone is even more pronounced in *España . . .* where Vallejo becomes a prophet and the two fundamental images are those of Christ's passion and the new Jerusalem. It is to be emphasized, however, that the poems deal not with a religious experience but with ordinary human experience and the religious terminology is applied not to the divinity but to humanity. It is man, not God, who is the divinity in Vallejo's religion.

Many of the techniques of *Trilce* are still to be found in *Poemas humanos*, but two predominate: reiteration and enumeration, and the use of various conceptual devices. The first seems to point to the influence of Whitman and the Bible, while the second seems to suggest the influence of Spanish classical writers, particularly Quevedo. Vallejo tends to insist on words and ideas and reiteration assumes a variety of forms. Sometimes a word qualifies itself or another word of the same root: "mi cosa cosa" (p. 127); "la pobre pobrecita" (p. 143). In other cases a word is reinforced by its synonym: "la tiniebla tenebrosa" (p. 145); "tú sufres, tú padeces" (p. 145). Words are often repeated in a series, usually with variants: "le ha dolido el dolor, el dolor joven, / el dolor niño, el dolorazo" (p. 142). Reiteration may involve the insistent repetition of a formula in the manner of a litany, as we have already seen. Sometimes an expression repeatedly reappears throughout a poem like the central theme in a musical composition: *Va corriendo, andando* . . . (p. 125) is constructed around the verb *huir* which is repeated eleven times. In *Los desgraciados* (p. 150) the *leit-motiv* "Ya va a venir el día" also reappears eleven times.

Vallejo also frequently employs the technique of "chaotic enumeration", though in his case it would be more exact to speak of reiterative enumeration, since it almost always has a reiterative function. It involves the accumulation of series of words and images: ". . . hubo tanto dolor en el pecho, en la solapa, en la cartera, / en el vaso, en la carnicería, en la aritmética!" (p. 134); ". . . en prototipo del alarde fálico, / en diabetes y en blanca vacinica, / en rostro geométrico, en difunto" (p. 137). Often enumeration takes the form of the repetition of a grammatical construction: ". . . por qué tiene la vida este perrazo, / por qué lloro, por qué / . . . hube nacido gritando" (p. 128). One form of enumeration might be called panegyric, since its function is to exalt. It is to be found mainly in *España* . . . : "Se amarán todos los hombres / y comerán . . . y beberán . . . Descansarán . . . sollozarán . . . venturosos serán . . . ajustarán . . . sus quehaceres . . . !" (*Himno*, ll. 90–98) (p. 163). In such cases the sound of the words often reinforces the sense: "Un día diurno, claro, atento, fértil" (p. 161).

Reiteration and enumeration sometimes determine the structure of a poem. Thus *Un hombre pasa* . . . (p. 146) and *¿ Qué me da* . . . *?* (p. 154) are made up of reiterative couplets. *Considerando en frío* . . . (p. 139) accumulates evidence proving man's insignificance.

The second basic technique is the use of the various conceptual devices that we have already noted in *Trilce*: antithesis, oxymoron and paradox. A word tends to evoke its opposite almost automatically: "al rey del vino, al esclavo del agua" (p. 149). Similarly *día* gives rise to *noche*, *vida* to *muerte*, *bien* to *mal*, *calor* to *frío*, etc. This juxtaposition of opposites assumes many forms. A verb may have a complement expressing the opposite idea: "proso / estos versos" (p. 143). Two contradictory nouns may be linked by a possessive: "el odio de este amor" (p. 126); "frío del calor". A noun may be qualified by an adjective expressing the opposite idea: "pobre rico" (p. 141); "frío incendio". An adverb or adverbial expression may modify a verb in the same way: ". . . el instinto de inmovilidad con que ando" (p. 138); "le odio con afecto" (p. 140). These verbal oppositions sometimes determine the whole structure of a poem. Thus *¿ Qué me da* . . . *?* (p. 154) is made up of couplets in which the last term of the second line opposes the last term of the first. Those stanzas which do not conform exactly to this pattern contain some element of opposition within them. It is important to remember, however, that these verbal oppositions are not gratuitous. Nor are they simply automatic. They are the result of the poet's obsession with the contradictions inherent in life and they presuppose a conscious poetic technique. They serve to reveal an absurd universe in a state of contradiction, a universe whose various elements are in conflict. In the poems of affirmation they serve the opposite function: they translate a new reality in which all opposites have been reconciled and all contradictions resolved.

Examples of paradox also abound: "parado / de tanto huir" (p. 125); "nació de puro humilde el Grande" (p. 144); "cautivo en tu enorme libertad" (p. 146); "Hasta cuando leamos, ignoran-tes!" (p. 148). These shock the reader into a greater understand-ing of the nature of reality and serve a function similar to the juxtaposition of opposites.

A feature of *Poemas humanos* is the great sense of rhythm demonstrated by Vallejo. Though the verse is still free, certain types of line—the hendecasyllable and the heptasyllable—tend to predominate. At the same time there is a greater concern for harmony and symmetry. Vallejo returns to more regular forms in poems like *Intensidad y altura* (p. 133). Poems like ¿ *Qué me da . . . ?* (p. 154) and *Un hombre pasa . . .* (p. 146) are made up of couplets. *Considerando en frío . . .* (p. 139), *Altura y pelos* (p. 154) and ¡ *Y si después de tantas palabras . . . ¡* (p. 155) are based on parallelisms. *Leit-motivs* play an important part in many poems such as *Los desgraciados* (p. 150), while the poet shows a particular liking for parallel lines: "aquesos tuyos pasos metalúrgicos, / aquesos tuyos pasos de otra vida" (p. 129). In addition the techniques of reiteration and enumeration which he uses systematically help create a rhythm. This rhythmical quality is one of the factors which signal the maturity of Vallejo's final book.

BIBLIOGRAPHY

1. VALLEJO'S WORKS

Obra poética completa, Moncloa, Lima, 1968.
Novelas y cuentos completos, Moncloa, Lima, 1967.
Rusia en 1931. Reflexiones al pie del Kremlin, Labor, Lima, 1965.
Rusia ante el segundo plan quinquenal, Labor, Lima, 1965.
El romanticismo en la poesía castellana, Mejía Baca & Villanueva, Lima, 1955.

2. BASIC WORKS ON VALLEJO

ANDRÉ COYNÉ, *César Vallejo y su obra poética*, Edit. Letras Peruanas, Lima, 1958.
JUAN ESPEJO ASTURRIZAGA, *César Vallejo. Itinerario del hombre*, Mejía Baca, Lima, 1965.
GIOVANNI MEO ZILIO, *Stile e poesia in César Vallejo*, Liviana, Padua, 1960.
LUIS MONGUIÓ, *César Vallejo (1892–1938). Vida y Obra. Bibliografía. Antología*, Hispanic Institute in the United States, New York, 1952. This was published in the *Revista Hispánica Moderna* in the same year.
ROBERTO PAOLI, *Poesie, di César Vallejo*, Lerici, Milan, 1964.
Also basic are the various numbers of the research review *Aula Vallejo*, Universidad Nacional de Córdoba, Argentina: 1, 1961; 2–4, 1962; 5–7, 1967.

3. SECONDARY BOOKS OF CRITICISM

XAVIER ABRIL, *Vallejo. Ensayo de aproximación crítica*, Front, Buenos Aires, 1958.
XAVIER ABRIL, *César Vallejo o la teoría poética*, Taurus, Madrid, 1962.
CÉSAR A. ANGELES CABALLERO, *César Vallejo. Su obra*, Minerva, Lima, 1964.
JUAN LARREA, *César Vallejo o Hispanoamérica en la cruz de su razón*, Universidad Nacional de Córdoba, Argentina, 1958.
MARIO JORGE DE LELLIS, *César Vallejo*, Edit. La Mandrágora, Buenos Aires, 1960.
LUIS MONGUIÓ, *La poesía postmodernista peruana*, Fondo de Cultura Económica, Mexico City, 1954.
ANTENOR SAMANIEGO, *César Vallejo, su poesía*, Mejía Baca, Lima, 1954.
SAÚL YURKIEVICH, *Valoración de Vallejo*, Universidad Nacional del Nordeste, Resistencia, Argentina, 1958.

4. ARTICLES AND ESSAYS

ALFREDO CARDONA PEÑA, 'Un soneto de César Vallejo', in *Cabral y Vallejo*, Colec. N. Ramicone, Buenos Aires, 1960, pp. 13–30.

MARIO CASTRO ARENAS, 'Algunos rasgos estilísticos de la poesía de César Vallejo', in *De Palma a Vallejo*, Populibros peruanos, Lima, 1964, pp. 7–39.

ALBERTO ESCOBAR, 'Símbolos en la poesía de Vallejo', in *Patio de Letras*, Caballo de Troya, Lima, 1965, pp. 258–81.

ALBERTO FERNÁNDEZ LEYS, 'Dimensión y destino de César Vallejo', *Universidad*, Universidad Nacional del Litoral, Santa Fe, Argentina, No. 51, 1962, pp. 69–105.

AMÉRICO FERRARI, 'César Vallejo. Trajectoire du poète', in *César Vallejo*, Poètes d'aujourd'hui, Seghers, Paris, 1967, pp. 5–59.

EUGENIO FLORIT, 'César Vallejo', in *The Poem Itself*, Ed. S. BURNSHAW, Pelican, London, 1964, pp. 220–7.

JAMES HIGGINS, 'The conflict of personality in César Vallejo's *Poemas humanos*', *Bulletin of Hispanic Studies*, xliii. 1, 1966, pp. 47–55.

JAMES HIGGINS, '*Los nueve monstruos* de César Vallejo: una tentativa de interpretación', *Razón y fábula*, Universidad de los Andes, Bogotá, 3, 1967, pp. 20–25.

JAMES HIGGINS, 'La posición religiosa de César Vallejo a través de su poesía', *Caravelle*, Toulouse, 9, 1967, pp. 47–58.

JAMES HIGGINS, 'Vallejo en cada poema', *Mundo Nuevo*, Paris, 22, 1968, pp. 21–26.

GIOVANNI MEO ZILIO and others, 'Neologismos en la poesía de César Vallejo', *Lavori della Sezione Fiorentina del Gruppo Ispanistico C.N.R.*, Casa Editrice G. D'Anna, Florence, 1967, Serie I, pp. 11–98.

LUIS MONGUIÓ, 'Muerte y poesía: España, 1936–1939', in *Estudios sobre literatura hispanoamericana y española*, Andrea, Col. Studium, Mexico City, 1958, pp. 169–81.

ALDO P. OLIVA, '*Trilce* de César Vallejo. Poema XXIII', *Boletín de Literaturas Hispánicas*, Universidad Nacional del Litoral, Argentina, 1, 1959, pp. 39–44.

JULIO ORTEGA, 'Una poética de *Trilce*', *Mundo Nuevo*, Paris, 22, 1968, pp. 26–29.

ALAIN SICARD, 'Sur le poème de César Vallejo: *Los Desgraciados*', *Caravelle*, Toulouse, 8, 1967, pp. 79–95.

SAÚL YURKIEVICH, 'En torno de *Trilce*', *Revista peruana de cultura*, Lima, 9–10, 1966, pp. 74–91.

ALONSO ZAMORA VICENTE, 'Considerando, comprendiendo. Notas a un poema de César Vallejo', in *Voz de la letra*, Espasa Calpe, Col. Austral No. 1287, Madrid, pp. 109–17.

ARMANDO ZUBIZARRETA, 'La cárcel en la poesía de César Vallejo', *Sphinx*, Lima, 13, 1960, pp. 214–21.

ANTHOLOGY

LOS HERALDOS NEGROS (1919)

Los heraldos negros

Hay golpes en la vida, tan fuertes . . . Yo no sé!
Golpes como del odio de Dios; como si ante ellos,
la resaca de todo lo sufrido
se empozara en el alma . . . Yo no sé!

Son pocos; pero son . . . Abren zanjas oscuras   5
en el rostro más fiero y en el lomo más fuerte.
Serán tal vez los potros de bárbaros atilas;
o los heraldos negros que nos manda la Muerte.

Son las caídas hondas de los Cristos del alma,
de alguna fe adorable que el Destino blasfema.   10
Esos golpes sangrientos son las crepitaciones
de algún pan que en la puerta del horno se nos quema.

Y el hombre . . . Pobre . . . pobre! Vuelve los ojos, como
cuando por sobre el hombro nos llama una palmada;
vuelve los ojos locos, y todo lo vivido   15
se empoza, como charco de culpa, en la mirada.

Hay golpes en la vida, tan fuertes . . . Yo no sé!

Setiembre

Aquella noche de setiembre, fuiste
tan buena para mí . . . hasta dolerme!
Yo no sé lo demás; y para eso,
no debiste ser buena, no debiste.

Aquella noche sollozaste al verme   5
hermético y tirano, enfermo y triste.
Yo no sé lo demás . . . y para eso,
yo no sé por qué fui triste . . . tan triste . . . !

Sólo esa noche de setiembre dulce,
10   tuve a tus ojos de Magdala, toda
la distancia de Dios . . . y te fui dulce!

Y también fue una tarde de setiembre
cuando sembré en tus brasas, desde un auto,
los charcos de esta noche de diciembre.

Heces

Esta tarde llueve, como nunca; y no
tengo ganas de vivir, corazón.

Esta tarde es dulce. Por qué no ha de ser?
Viste gracia y pena; viste de mujer.

5   Esta tarde en Lima llueve. Y yo recuerdo
las cavernas crueles de mi ingratitud;
mi bloque de hielo sobre su amapola,
más fuerte que su "No seas así!"

Mis violentas flores negras; y la bárbara
10   y enorme pedrada; y el trecho glacial.
Y pondrá el silencio de su dignidad
con óleos quemantes el punto final.

Por eso esta tarde, como nunca, voy
con este búho, con este corazón.

15   Y otras pasan; y viéndome tan triste,
toman un poquito de ti
en la abrupta arruga de mi hondo dolor.

Esta tarde llueve, llueve mucho. ¡ Y no
tengo ganas de vivir, corazón !

Ágape

Hoy no ha venido nadie a preguntar;
ni me han pedido en esta tarde nada.

No he visto ni una flor de cementerio
en tan alegre procesión de luces.
Perdóname, Señor: qué poco he muerto!   5

En esta tarde todos, todos pasan
sin preguntarme ni pedirme nada.

Y no sé qué se olvidan y se queda
mal en mis manos, como cosa ajena.

He salido a la puerta,   10
y me da ganas de gritar a todos:
Si echan de menos algo, aquí se queda!

Porque en todas las tardes de esta vida,
yo no sé con qué puertas dan a un rostro,
y algo ajeno se toma el alma mía.   15

Hoy no ha venido nadie;
y hoy he muerto qué poco en esta tarde!

La de a mil

El suertero que grita "La de a mil",
contiene no sé qué fondo de Dios.

Pasan todos los labios. El hastío
despunta en una arruga su yanó.
Pasa el suertero que atesora, acaso   5
nominal, como Dios,
entre panes tantálicos, humana
impotencia de amor.

Yo le miro al andrajo. Y él pudiera
10   darnos el corazón;
pero la suerte aquella que en sus manos
aporta, pregonando en alta voz,
como un pájaro cruel, irá a parar
adonde no lo sabe ni lo quiere
15   este bohemio dios.

Y digo en este viernes tibio que anda
a cuestas bajo el sol:
¡ por qué se habrá vestido de suertero
la voluntad de Dios !

El pan nuestro

Se bebe el desayuno . . . Húmeda tierra
de cementerio huele a sangre amada.
Ciudad de invierno . . . La mordaz cruzada
de una carreta que arrastrar parece
5   una emoción de ayuno encadenada!

Se quisiera tocar todas las puertas,
y preguntar por no sé quién; y luego
ver a los pobres, y, llorando quedos,
dar pedacitos de pan fresco a todos.
10   Y saquear a los ricos sus viñedos
con las dos manos santas
que a un golpe de luz
volaron desclavadas de la Cruz!

Pestaña matinal, no os levantéis!
15   ¡ El pan nuestro de cada día dánoslo,
Señor . . . !

Todos mis huesos son ajenos;
yo talvez los robé!

Yo vine a darme lo que acaso estuvo
asignado para otro;   20
y pienso que, si no hubiera nacido,
otro pobre tomara este café!
Yo soy un mal ladrón . . . A dónde iré!

Y en esta hora fría, en que la tierra
trasciende a polvo humano y es tan triste,   25
quisiera yo tocar todas las puertas,
y suplicar a no sé quién, perdón,
y hacerle pedacitos de pan fresco
aquí, en el horno de mi corazón . . . !

Absoluta

Color de ropa antigua. Un julio a sombra,
y un agosto recién segado. Y una
mano de agua que injertó en el pino
resinoso de un tedio malas frutas.

Ahora que has anclado, oscura ropa,   5
tornas rociada de un suntuoso olor
a tiempo, a abreviación . . . Y he cantado
el proclive festín que se volcó.

Mas ¿ no puedes, Señor, contra la muerte,
contra el límite, contra lo que acaba?   10
Ay! la llaga en color de ropa antigua,
cómo se entreabre y huele a miel quemada!

Oh unidad excelsa! Oh lo que es uno
por todos!
Amor contra el espacio y contra el tiempo!   15
Un latido único de corazón;
un solo ritmo: Dios!

Y al encogerse de hombros los linderos
en un bronco desdén irreductible,
20   hay un riego de sierpes
en la doncella plenitud del l.
¡ Una arruga, una sombra!

Líneas

Cada cinta de fuego
que, en busca del Amor,
arrojo y vibra en rosas lamentables,
me da a luz el sepelio de una víspera.
5   Yo no sé si el redoble en que lo busco,
será jadear de roca,
o perenne nacer de corazón.

Hay tendida hacia el fondo de los seres,
un eje ultranervioso, honda plomada.
10   ¡ La hebra del destino!
Amor desviará tal ley de vida,
hacia la voz del Hombre;
y nos dará la libertad suprema
en transubstanciación azul, virtuosa,
15   contra lo ciego y lo fatal.

¡ Que en cada cifra lata,
recluso en albas frágiles,
el Jesús aún mejor de otra gran Yema!

Y después . . . La otra línea . . .
20   Un Bautista que aguaita, aguaita, aguaita . . .
Y, cabalgando en intangible curva,
un pie bañado en púrpura.

La cena miserable

Hasta cuándo estaremos esperando lo que
no se nos debe . . . Y en qué recodo estiraremos
nuestra pobre rodilla para siempre! Hasta cuándo
la cruz que nos alienta no detendrá sus remos.

Hasta cuándo la Duda nos brindará blasones   5
por haber padecido . . .
                              Ya nos hemos sentado
mucho a la mesa, con la amargura de un niño
que a media noche, llora de hambre, desvelado . . .

Y cuándo nos veremos con los demás, al borde   10
de una mañana eterna, desayunados todos.
Hasta cuándo este valle de lágrimas, a donde
yo nunca dije que me trajeran.
                        De codos
todo bañado en llanto, repito cabizbajo   15
y vencido: hasta cuándo la cena durará.

Hay alguien que ha bebido mucho, y se burla,
y acerca y aleja de nosotros, como negra cuchara
de amarga esencia humana, la tumba . . .
                              Y menos sabe   20
ese oscuro hasta cuándo la cena durará!

Los dados eternos

Dios mío, estoy llorando el ser que vivo;
me pesa haber tomádote tu pan;
pero este pobre barro pensativo
no es costra fermentada en tu costado:
tú no tienes Marías que se van!   5

Dios mío, si tú hubieras sido hombre,
hoy supieras ser Dios;
pero tú, que estuviste siempre bien,
no sientes nada de tu creación.
10   Y el hombre sí te sufre: el Dios es él!

Hoy que en mis ojos brujos hay candelas,
como en un condenado,
Dios mío, prenderás todas tus velas,
y jugaremos con el viejo dado . . .
15   Talvez ¡ oh jugador! al dar la suerte
del universo todo,
surgirán las ojeras de la Muerte,
como dos ases fúnebres de lodo.

Dios mío, y esta noche sorda, oscura,
20   ya no podrás jugar, porque la Tierra
es un dado roído y ya redondo
a fuerza de rodar a la aventura,
que no puede parar sino en un hueco,
en el hueco de inmensa sepultura.

Los anillos fatigados

Hay ganas de volver, de amar, de no ausentarse,
y hay ganas de morir, combatido por dos
aguas encontradas que jamás han de istmarse.

Hay ganas de un gran beso que amortaje a la Vida,
5   que acaba en el áfrica de una agonía ardiente,
suicida!

Hay ganas de . . . no tener ganas, Señor;
a ti yo te señalo con el dedo deicida;
hay ganas de no haber tenido corazón.

La primavera vuelve, vuelve y se irá. Y Dios,   10
curvado en tiempo, se repite, y pasa, pasa
a cuestas con la espina dorsal del Universo.

Cuando las sienes tocan su lúgubre tambor,
cuando me duele el sueño grabado en un puñal,
¡ hay ganas de quedarse plantado en este verso!   15

Dios

Siento a Dios que camina
tan en mí, con la tarde y con el mar.
Con él nos vamos juntos. Anochece.
Con él anochecemos. Orfandad . . .

Pero yo siento a Dios. Y hasta parece   5
que él me dicta no sé qué buen color.
Como un hospitalario, es bueno y triste;
mustia un dulce desdén de enamorado:
debe dolerle mucho el corazón.

Oh, Dios mío, recién a ti me llego,   10
hoy que amo tanto en esta tarde; hoy
que en la falsa balanza de unos senos,
mido y lloro una frágil Creación.

Y tú, cuál llorarás . . . tú, enamorado
de tanto enorme seno girador . . .   15
Yo te consagro Dios, porque amas tanto;
porque jamás sonríes; porque siempre
debe dolerte mucho el corazón.

Los pasos lejanos

Mi padre duerme. Su semblante augusto
figura un apacible corazón;
está ahora tan dulce . . .
si hay algo en él de amargo, seré yo.

5   Hay soledad en el hogar; se reza;
y no hay noticias de los hijos hoy.
Mi padre se despierta, ausculta
la huída a Egipto, el restañante adiós.
Está ahora tan cerca;
10 si hay algo en él de lejos, seré yo.

   Y mi madre pasea allá en los huertos,
saboreando un sabor ya sin sabor.
Está ahora tan suave,
tan ala, tan salida, tan amor.

15   Hay soledad en el hogar sin bulla,
sin noticias, sin verde, sin niñez.
Y si hay algo quebrado en esta tarde,
y que baja y que cruje,
son dos viejos caminos blancos, curvos.
20 Por ellos va mi corazón a pie.

    A mi hermano Miguel

       In memoriam

  Hermano, hoy estoy en el poyo de la casa,
donde nos haces una falta sin fondo!
Me acuerdo que jugábamos esta hora, y que mamá
nos acariciaba: "Pero, hijos . . ."

5   Ahora yo me escondo,
como antes, todas estas oraciones
vespertinas, y espero que tú no des conmigo.
Por la sala, el zaguán, los corredores.
Después, te ocultas tú, y yo no doy contigo.
10 Me acuerdo que nos hacíamos llorar,
hermano, en aquel juego.

Miguel, tú te escondiste
una noche de agosto, al alborear;
pero, en vez de ocultarte riendo, estabas triste.
Y tu gemelo corazón de esas tardes   15
extintas se ha aburrido de no encontrarte. Y ya
cae sombra en el alma.

Oye, hermano, no tardes
en salir. Bueno? Puede inquietarse mamá.

Enereida

Mi padre, apenas,
en la mañana pajarina, pone
sus setentiocho años, sus setentiocho
ramos de invierno a solear.
El cementerio de Santiago, untado   5
en alegre año nuevo, está a la vista.
Cuántas veces sus pasos cortaron hacia él,
y tornaron de algún entierro humilde.

Hoy hace mucho tiempo que mi padre no sale!
Una broma de niños se desbanda.   10

Otras veces le hablaba a mi madre
de impresiones urbanas, de política;
y hoy, apoyado en su bastón ilustre
que sonara mejor en los años de la Gobernación,
mi padre está desconocido, frágil,   15
mi padre es una víspera.
Lleva, trae, abstraído, reliquias, cosas,
recuerdos, sugerencias.
La mañana apacible le acompaña
con sus alas blancas de hermana de caridad.   20

Día eterno es éste, día ingenuo, infante,
coral, oracional;
se corona el tiempo de palomas,
y el futuro se puebla
25   de caravanas de inmortales rosas.
Padre, aún sigue todo despertando;
es enero que canta, es tu amor
que resonando va en la Eternidad.
Aún reirás de tus pequeñuelos,
30   y habrá bulla triunfal en los Vacíos.

Aún será año nuevo. Habrá empanadas;
y yo tendré hambre, cuando toque a misa
en el beato campanario
el buen ciego mélico con quien
35   departieron mis sílabas escolares y frescas,
mi inocencia rotunda.
Y cuando la mañana llena de gracia,
desde sus senos de tiempo
que son dos renuncias, dos avances de amor
40   que se tienden y ruegan infinito, eterna vida,
cante, y eche a volar Verbos plurales,
jirones de tu ser,
a la borda de sus alas blancas
de hermana de caridad ¡ oh, padre mío!

Espergesia

Yo nací un día
que Dios estuvo enfermo.

Todos saben que vivo,
que soy malo; y no saben
5   del diciembre de ese enero.
Pues yo nací un día
que Dios estuvo enfermo.

Hay un vacío
en mi aire metafísico
que nadie ha de palpar: 10
el claustro de un silencio
que habló a flor de fuego.
Yo nací un día
que Dios estuvo enfermo.

Hermano, escucha, escucha . . .   15
Bueno. Y que no me vaya
sin llevar diciembres,
sin dejar eneros.
Pues yo nací un día
que Dios estuvo enfermo.   20

Todos saben que vivo,
que mastico . . . Y no saben
por qué en mi verso chirrian,
oscuro sinsabor de féretro,
luyidos vientos   25
desenroscados de la Esfinge
preguntona del Desierto.

Todos saben . . . Yo no saben
que la Luz es tísica,
y la Sombra gorda . . .   30
Y no saben que el Misterio sintetiza . . .
que él es la joroba
musical y triste que a distancia denuncia
el paso meridiano de las lindes a las Lindes.

Yo nací un día   35
que Dios estuvo enfermo,
grave.

TRILCE (1922)

III

Las personas mayores
¿ a qué hora volverán?
Da las seis el ciego Santiago,
y ya está muy oscuro.

Madre dijo que no demoraría.   5

Aguedita, Nativa, Miguel,
cuidado con ir por ahí, por donde
acaban de pasar gangueando sus memorias
dobladoras penas,
hacia el silencioso corral, y por donde   10
las gallinas que se están acostando todavía,
se han espantado tanto.
Mejor estemos aquí no más.
Madre dijo que no demoraría.

Ya no tengamos pena. Vamos viendo   15
los barcos ¡ el mío es más bonito de todos!
con los cuales jugamos todo el santo día,
sin pelearnos, como debe de ser:
han quedado en el pozo de agua, listos,
fletados de dulces para mañana.   20

Aguardemos así, obedientes y sin más
remedio, la vuelta, el desagravio
de los mayores siempre delanteros
dejándonos en casa a los pequeños,
como si también nosotros   25
                    no pudiésemos partir.

Aguedita, Nativa, Miguel?
Llamo, busco al tanteo en la oscuridad.
No me vayan a haber dejado solo,
30   y el único recluso sea yo.

V

Grupo dicotiledón. Oberturan
desde él petreles, propensiones de trinidad,
finales que comienzan, ohs de ayes
creyérase avaloriados de heterogeneidad.
5   ¡ Grupo de los dos cotiledones!

A ver. Aquello sea sin ser más.
A ver. No trascienda hacia afuera,
y piense en son de no ser escuchado,
y crome y no sea visto.
10   Y no glise en el gran colapso.

La creada voz rebélase y no quiere
ser malla, ni amor.
Los novios sean novios en eternidad.
Pues no deis 1, que resonará al infinito.
15   Y no deis 0, que callará tanto,
hasta despertar y poner de pie al 1.

Ah grupo bicardiaco.

VI

El traje que vestí mañana
no lo ha lavado mi lavandera:
lo lavaba en sus venas otilinas,
en el chorro de su corazón, y hoy no he
5   de preguntarme si yo dejaba
el traje turbio de injusticia.

A hora que no hay quien vaya a las aguas,
en mis falsillas encañona
el lienzo para emplumar, y todas las cosas
del velador de tanto qué será de mí,   10
todas no están mías
a mi lado.

                        Quedaron de su propiedad,
fratesadas, selladas con su trigueña bondad.

Y si supiera si ha de volver;   15
y si supiera qué mañana entrará
a entregarme las ropas lavadas, mi aquella
lavandera del alma. Qué mañana entrará
satisfecha, capulí de obrería, dichosa
de probar que sí sabe, que sí puede   20
              ¡ CÓMO NO VA A PODER!
azular y planchar todos los caos.

XV

En el rincón aquel, donde dormimos juntos
tantas noches, ahora me he sentado
a caminar. La cuja de los novios difuntos
fue sacada, o talvez qué habrá pasado.

Has venido temprano a otros asuntos   5
y ya no estás. Es el rincón
donde a tu lado, leí una noche,
entre tus tiernos puntos,
un cuento de Daudet. Es el rincón
amado. No lo equivoques.   10

Me he puesto a recordar los días
de verano idos, tu entrar y salir,
poca y harta y pálida por los cuartos.

En esta noche pluviosa,
15   ya lejos de ambos dos, salto de pronto . . .
Son dos puertas abriéndose cerrándose,
dos puertas que al viento van y vienen
sombra   a   sombra.

XVIII

Oh las cuatro paredes de la celda,
Ah las cuatro paredes albicantes
que sin remedio dan al mismo número.

Criadero de nervios, mala brecha,
5   por sus cuatro rincones cómo arranca
las diarias aherrojadas extremidades.

Amorosa llavera de innumerables llaves,
si estuvieras aquí, si vieras hasta
qué hora son cuatro estas paredes.
10   Contra ellas seríamos contigo, los dos,
más dos que nunca. Y ni lloraras,
di, libertadora!

Ah las paredes de la celda.
De ellas me duelen entretanto más
15   las dos largas que tienen esta noche
algo de madres que ya muertas
llevan por bromurados declives,
a un niño de la mano cada una.

Y sólo yo me voy quedando,
20   con la diestra, que hace por ambas manos,
en alto, en busca de terciario brazo
que ha de pupilar, entre mi donde y mi cuando,
esta mayoría inválida de hombre.

XIX

A trastear, Hélpide dulce, escampas,
cómo quedamos de tan quedarnos.

Hoy vienes apenas me he levantado.
El establo está divinamente meado
y excrementido por la vaca inocente   5
y el inocente asno y el gallo inocente.

Penetra en la maría ecuménica.
Oh sangabriel, haz que conciba el alma,
el sin luz amor, el sin cielo,
lo más piedra, lo más nada,   10
                hasta la ilusión monarca.

Quemaremos todas las naves!
Quemaremos la última esencia!

Mas si se ha de sufrir de mito a mito,
y a hablarme llegas masticando hielo,   15
mastiquemos brasas,
ya no hay dónde bajar,
ya no hay dónde subir.

Se ha puesto el gallo incierto, hombre.

XXI

En un auto arteriado de círculos viciosos,
torna diciembre qué cambiado,
con su oro en desgracia. Quién le viera:
diciembre con sus 31 pieles rotas,
                    el pobre diablo.   5

Yo le recuerdo. Hubimos de esplendor,
bocas ensortijadas de mal engreimiento,
todas arrastrando recelos infinitos.
Cómo no voy a recordarle
10 al magro señor Doce.

Yo le recuerdo. Y hoy diciembre torna
qué cambiado, el aliento a infortunio,
helado, moqueando humillación.

Y a la ternurosa avestruz
15 como que la ha querido, como que la ha adorado.
Por ella se ha calzado todas sus diferencias.

XXII

Es posible me persigan hasta cuatro
magistrados vuelto. Es posible me juzguen pedro.
¡Cuatro humanidades justas juntas!
Don Juan Jacobo está en hacerio,
5 y las burlas le tiran de su soledad,
como a un tonto. Bien hecho.

Farol rotoso, el día induce a darle algo,
y pende
a modo de asterisco que se mendiga
10 a sí propio quizás qué enmendaturas.

Ahora que chirapa tan bonito
en esta paz de una sola línea,
aquí me tienes,
aquí me tienes, de quien yo penda,
15 para que sacies mis esquinas.
Y si, éstas colmadas,
te derramases de mayor bondad,
sacaré de donde no haya,

forjaré de locura otros posillos,
insaciables ganas   20
de nivel y amor.

Si pues siempre salimos al encuentro
de cuanto entra por otro lado,
ahora, chirapado eterno y todo,
heme, de quien yo penda,   25
estoy de filo todavía. Heme!

XXIII

Tahona estuosa de aquellos mis bizcochos
pura yema infantil innumerable, madre.

Oh tus cuatro gorgas, asombrosamente
mal plañidas, madre: tus mendigos.
Las dos hermanas últimas, Miguel que ha muerto   5
y yo arrastrando todavía
una trenza por cada letra del abecedario.

En la sala de arriba nos repartías
de mañana, de tarde, de dual estiba,
aquellas ricas hostias de tiempo, para   10
que ahora nos sobrasen
cáscaras de relojes en flexión de las 24
en punto parados.

Madre, y ahora! Ahora, en cuál alvéolo
quedaría, en qué retoño capilar,   15
cierta migaja que hoy se me ata al cuello
y no quiere pasar. Hoy que hasta
tus puros huesos estarán harina
que no habrá en qué amasar
¡tierna dulcera de amor!,   20

hasta en la cruda sombra, hasta en el gran molar
cuya encía late en aquel lácteo hoyuelo
que inadvertido lábrase y pulula ¡ tú lo viste tanto!
en las cerradas manos recién nacidas.

25 Tal la tierra oirá en tu silenciar,
cómo nos van cobrando todos
el alquiler del mundo donde nos dejas
y el valor de aquel pan inacabable.
Y nos lo cobran, cuando, siendo nosotros
30 pequeños entonces, como tú verías,
no se lo podíamos haber arrebatado
a nadie; cuando tú nos lo diste,
¿ di, mamá?

XXVIII

He almorzado solo ahora, y no he tenido
madre, ni súplica, ni sírvete, ni agua,
ni padre que, en el facundo ofertorio
de los choclos, pregunte para su tardanza
5 de imagen, por los broches mayores del sonido.

Cómo iba yo a almorzar. Cómo me iba a servir
de tales platos distantes esas cosas,
cuando habráse quebrado el propio hogar,
cuando no asoma ni madre a los labios.
10 Cómo iba yo a almorzar nonada.

A la mesa de un buen amigo he almorzado
con su padre recién llegado del mundo,
con sus canas tías que hablan
en tordillo retinte de porcelana,
15 bisbiseando por todos sus viudos alvéolos;
y con cubiertos francos de alegres tiroriros,

porque estánse en su casa. Así, qué gracia!
Y me han dolido los cuchillos
de esta mesa en todo el paladar.

El yantar de estas mesas así, en que se prueba   20
amor ajeno en vez del propio amor,
torna tierra el bocado que no brinda la
                    MADRE,
hace golpe la dura deglusión; el dulce,
hiel; aceite funéreo, el café.   25

Cuando ya se ha quebrado el propio hogar,
y el sírvete materno no sale de la
tumba,
la cocina a oscuras, la miseria de amor.

XXXIII

Si lloviera esta noche, retiraríame
de aquí a mil años.
Mejor a cien no más.
Como si nada hubiese ocurrido, haría
la cuenta de que vengo todavía.   5

O sin madre, sin amada, sin porfía
de agacharme a aguaitar al fondo, a puro
pulso,
esta noche así, estaría escarmenando
la fibra védica,   10
la lana védica de mi fin final, hilo
del diantre, traza de haber tenido
por las narices
a dos badajos inacordes de tiempo
        en una misma campana.   15

Haga la cuenta de mi vida
o haga la cuenta de no haber aún nacido,
no alcanzaré a librarme.

No será lo que aún no haya venido, sino
20 lo que ha llegado y ya se ha ido,
sino lo que ha llegado y ya se ha ido.

XXXV

El encuentro con la amada
tanto alguna vez, es un simple detalle,
casi un programa hípico en violado,
que de tan largo no se puede doblar bien.

5 El almuerzo con ella que estaría
poniendo el plato que nos gustara ayer
y se repite ahora,
pero con algo más de mostaza;
el tenedor absorto, su doneo radiante
10 de pistilo en mayo, y su verecundia
de a centavito, por quítame allá esa paja.
Y la cerveza lírica y nerviosa
a la que celan sus dos pezones sin lúpulo,
y que no se debe tomar mucho!

15 Y los demás encantos de la mesa
que aquella núbil campaña borda
con sus propias baterías germinales
que han operado toda la mañana,
según me consta, a mí,
20 amoroso notario de sus intimidades,
y con las diez varillas mágicas
de sus dedos pancreáticos.

Mujer que, sin pensar en nada más allá,
suelta el mirlo y se pone a conversarnos
sus palabras tiernas   25
como lancinantes lechugas recién cortadas.

Otro vaso y me voy. Y nos marchamos,
ahora sí, a trabajar.

Entre tanto, ella se interna
entre los cortinajes y ¡ oh aguja de mis días   30
desgarrados! se sienta a la orilla
de una costura, a coserme el costado
a su costado,
a pegar el botón de esa camisa,
que se ha vuelto a caer. Pero hase visto!   35

XXXVI

Pugnamos ensartarnos por un ojo de aguja,
enfrentados, a las ganadas.
Amoniácase casi el cuarto ángulo del círculo.
¡ Hembra se continúa el macho, a raíz
de probables senos, y precisamente   5
a raíz de cuanto no florece!

¿ Por ahí estás, Venus de Milo?
Tú manqueas apenas pululando
entrañada en los brazos plenarios
de la existencia,   10
de esta existencia que todaviiza
perenne imperfección.
Venus de Milo, cuyo cercenado, increado
brazo revuélvese y trata de encodarse
a través de verdeantes guijarros gagos,   15

ortivos nautilos, aunes que gatean
recién, vísperas inmortales.
Laceadora de inminencias, laceadora
del paréntesis.

20   Rehusad, y vosotros, a posar las plantas
en la seguridad dupla de la Armonía.
Rehusad la simetría a buen seguro.
Intervenid en el conflicto
de puntas que se disputan
25   en la más torionda de las justas
el salto por el ojo de la aguja!

Tal siento ahora al meñique
demás en la siniestra. Lo veo y creo
no debe serme, o por lo menos que está
30   en sitio dondo no debe.
Y me inspira rabia y me azarea
y no hay cómo salir de él, sino haciendo
la cuenta de que hoy es jueves.

¡ Ceded al nuevo impar
35   potente de orfandad!

XXXVIII

Este cristal aguarda ser sorbido
en bruto por boca venidera
din dientes. No desdentada.
Este cristal es pan no venido todavía.

5   Hiere cuando lo fuerzan
y ya no tiene cariños animales.
Mas si se le apasiona, se melaría
y tomaría la horma de los sustantivos
que se adjetivan de brindarse.

Quienes lo ven allí triste individuo   10
incoloro, lo enviarían por amor,
por pasado y a lo más por futuro:
si él no dase por ninguno de sus costados;
se él espera ser sorbido de golpe
y en cuanto transparencia, por boca ve-   15
nidera que ya no tendrá dientes.

Este cristal ha pasado de animal,
y márchase ahora a formar las izquierdas,
los nuevos Menos.
Déjenlo solo no más.   20

XLV

Me desvinculo del mar
cuando vienen las aguas a mí.

Salgamos siempre. Saboreemos
la canción estupenda, la canción dicha
por los labios inferiores del deseo.   5
Oh prodigiosa doncellez.
Pasa la brisa sin sal.

A lo lejos husmeo los tuétanos
oyendo el tanteo profundo, a la caza
de teclas de resaca.   10

Y si así diéramos las narices
en el absurdo,
nos cubriremos con el oro de no tener nada,
y empollaremos el ala aún no nacida
de la noche, hermana   15
de esta ala huérfana del día,
que a fuerza de ser una ya no es ala.

XLVII

Ciliado arrecife donde nací,
según refieren cronicones y pliegos
de labios familiares historiados
en segunda gracia.

5   Ciliado archipiélago, te desislas a fondo,
              a fondo, archipiélago mío!
Duras todavía las articulaciones
al camino, como cuando nos instan
y nosotros no cedemos por nada.

10   Al ver los párpados cerrados,
implumes mayorcitos, decorando azules bombones,
se carcajean pericotes viejos.
Los párpados cerrados, como si, cuando, nacemos
siempre no fuese tiempo todavía.

15   Se va el altar, el cirio para
que no le pasase nada a mi madre,
y por mí que sería con los años, si Dios
quería, Obispo, Papa, Santo, o talvez
sólo un columnario dolor de cabeza.

20   Y las manitas que se abarquillan
asiéndose de algo flotante,
a no querer quedarse.
Y siendo ya la l.

LI

Mentira. Si lo hacía de engaños,
y nada más. Ya está. De otro modo,
también tú vas a ver
cuánto va a dolerme el haber sido así.

Mentira. Calla.   5
Ya está bien.
Como otras veces tú me haces esto mismo,
por eso yo también he sido así.

A mí, que había tanto atisbado si de veras
llorabas,   10
ya que otras veces sólo te quedaste
en tus dulces pucheros,
a mí, que ni soñé que los creyeses,
me ganaron tus lágrimas.
Ya está.   15

Mas ya lo sabes: todo fue mentira.
Y si sigues llorando, bueno, pues!
Otra vez ni he de verte cuando juegues.

LIII

Quién clama las once no son doce!
Como si las hubiesen pujado, se afrontan
de dos en dos las once veces.

Cabezazo brutal. Asoman
las coronas a oír,   5
pero sin traspasar los eternos
trescientos sesenta grados, asoman
y exploran en balde, dónde ambas manos
ocultan el otro puente que les nace
entre veras y litúrgicas bromas.   10

Vuelve la frontera a probar
las dos piedras que no alcanzan a ocupar
una misma posada a un mismo tiempo.
La frontera, la ambulante batuta, que sigue
inmutable, igual, sólo   15
más ella a cada esguince en alto.

Veis lo que es sin poder ser negado,
veis lo que tenemos que aguantar,
mal que nos pese.
20   ¡ Cuánto se aceita en codos
que llegan hasta la boca!

LVI

Todos los días amanezco a ciegas
a trabajar para vivir; y tomo el desayuno,
sin probar ni gota de él, todas las mañanas.
Sin saber si he logrado, o más nunca,
5   algo que brinca del sabor
o es sólo corazón y que ya vuelto, lamentará
hasta dónde esto es lo menos.

El niño crecería ahíto de felicidad
                oh albas,
10   ante el pesar de los padres de no poder dejarnos
de arrancar de sus sueños de amor a este mundo;
ante ellos que, como Dios, de tanto amor
se comprendieron hasta creadores
y nos quisieron hasta hacernos daño.

15   Flecos de invisible trama,
dientes que huronean desde la neutra emoción,
                pilares
libres de base y coronación,
en la gran boca que ha perdido el habla.

20   Fósforo y fósforo en la oscuridad,
lágrima y lágrima en la polvareda.

LVIII

En la celda, en lo sólido, también
se acurrucan los rincones.

Arreglo los desnudos que se ajan,
se doblan, se harapan.

Apéome del caballo jadeante, bufando   5
líneas de bofetadas y de horizontes;
espumoso pie contra tres cascos.
Y le ayudo: Anda, animal!

Se tomaría menos, siempre menos, de lo
que me tocase erogar,   10
en la celda, en lo líquido.

El compañero de prisión comía el trigo
de las lomas, con mi propia cuchara,
cuando, a la mesa de mis padres, niño,
me quedaba dormido masticando.   15

Le soplo al otro:
Vuelve, sal por la otra esquina;
apura . . . aprisa . . . apronta!

E inadvertido aduzco, planeo,
cabe camastro desvencijado, piadoso: 20
No creas. Aquel médico era un hombre sano.

Ya no reiré cuando mi madre rece
en infancia y en domingo, a las cuatro
de la madrugada, por los caminantes,
encarcelados,   25
enfermos
y pobres.

En el redil de niños, ya no le asestaré
puñetazos a ninguno de ellos, quien, después,
todavía sangrando, lloraría: El otro sábado   30

te daré mi fiambre, pero
no me pegues!
Ya no le diré que bueno.

En la celda, en el gas ilimitado
35   hasta redondearse en la condensación,
¿ quién tropieza por afuera?

LX

Es de madera mi paciencia,
sorda, vejetal.

Día que has sido puro, niño, inútil,
que naciste desnudo, las leguas
5   de tu marcha van corriendo sobre
tus doce extremidades, ese doblez ceñudo
que después deshiláchase
en no se sabe qué últimos pañales.

Constelado de hemisferios de grumo,
10   bajo eternas américas inéditas, tu gran plumaje,
te partes y me dejas, sin tu emoción ambigua,
sin tu nudo de sueños, domingo.

Y se apolilla mi paciencia,
y me vuelvo a exclamar: ¡ Cuándo vendrá
15   el domingo bocón y mudo del sepulcro;
cuándo vendrá a cargar este sábado
de harapos, esta horrible sutura
del placer que nos engendra sin querer,
y el placer que nos DestieRRa!

LXI

Esta noche desciendo del caballo,
ante la puerta de la casa, donde
me despedí con el cantar del gallo.
Está cerrada y nadie responde.

El poyo en que mamá alumbró   5
al hermano mayor, para que ensille
lomos que había yo montado en pelo,
por rúas y por cercas, niño aldeano;
el poyo en que dejé que se amarille al sol
mi adolorida infancia . . . ¿ Y este duelo   10
que enmarca la portada?

Dios en la paz foránea,
estornuda, cual llamando también, el bruto;
husmea, golpeando el empedrado. Luego duda,
relincha,   15
orejea a viva oreja.

Ha de velar papá rezando, y quizás
pensará se me hizo tarde.
Las hermanas, canturreando sus ilusiones
sencillas, bullosas,   20
en la labor para la fiesta que se acerca,
y ya no falta casi nada.
Espero, espero, el corazón
un huevo en su momento, que se obstruye.

Numerosa familia que dejamos   25
no ha mucho, hoy nadie en vela, y ni una cera
puso en el ara para que volviéramos.

Llamo de nuevo, y nada.
Callamos y nos ponemos a sollozar, y el animal
relincha, relincha más todavía.   30

Todos están durmiendo para siempre,
y tan de lo más bien, que por fin
mi caballo acaba fatigado por cabecear
a su vez, y entre sueños, a cada venia, dice
35   que está bien, que todo está muy bien.

LXV

Madre, me voy mañana a Santiago,
a mojarme en tu bendición y en tu llanto.
Acomodando estoy mis desengaños y el rosado
de llaga de mis falsos trajines.

5   Me esperará tu arco de asombro,
las tonsuradas columnas de tus ansias
que se acaban la vida. Me esperará el patio,
el corredor de abajo con sus tondos y repulgos
de fiesta. Me esperará mi sillón ayo,
10   aquel buen quijarudo trasto de dinástico
cuero, que para no más rezongando a las nalgas
tataranietas, de correa a correhuela.

Estoy cribando mis cariños más puros.
Estoy ejeando, ¿ no oyes jadear la sonda?
15   ¿ no oyes tascar dianas?
estoy plasmando tu fórmula de amor
para todos los huecos de este suelo.
Oh si se dispusieran los tácitos volantes
para todas las cintas más distantes,
20   para todas las citas más distintas.

Así, muerta inmortal. Así.
Bajo los dobles arcos de tu sangre, por donde
hay que pasar tan de puntillas, que hasta mi padre
para ir por allí,
25   humildóse hasta menos de la mitad del hombre,
hasta ser el primer pequeño que tuviste.

Así, muerta inmortal.
Entre la columnata de tus huesos
que no puede caer ni a lloros,
y a cuyo lado ni el Destino pudo entrometer   30
ni un solo dedo suyo.

Así, muerta inmortal.
Así.

LXXI

Serpea el sol en tu mano fresca,
y se derrama cauteloso en tu curiosidad.

Cállate. Nadie sabe que estás en mí,
toda entera. Cállate. No respires. Nadie
sabe mi merienda suculenta de unidad;   5
legión de oscuridades, amazonas de lloro.

Vanse los carros flagelados por la tarde,
y entre ellos los míos, cara atrás, a las riendas
fatales de tus dedos.
Tus manos y mis manos recíprocas se tienden   10
polos en guardia, practicando depresiones,
y sienes y costados.

Calla también, crepúsculo futuro,
y recógete a reír en lo íntimo, de este celo
de gallos ajisecos soberbiamente,   15
soberbiamente ennavajados
de cúpulas, de viudas mitades cerúleas.
Regocíjate, huérfano; bebe tu copa de agua
desde la pulpería de una esquina cualquiera.

LXXVI

De la noche a la mañana voy
sacando lengua a las más mudas equis.

En nombre de esa pura
que sabía mirar hasta ser 2.

En nombre de que la fui extraño,
llave y chapa muy diferentes.

En nombre della que no tuvo voz
ni voto, cuando se dispuso
esta su suerte de hacer.

Ebullición de cuerpos, sin embargo,
aptos; ebullición que siempre
tan sólo estuvo a 99 burbujas.

¡ Remates, esposados en naturaleza,
de dos días que no se juntan,
que no se alcanzan jamás!

LXXVII

Graniza tanto, como para que yo recuerde
y acreciente las perlas
que he recogido del hocico mismo
de cada tempestad.

No se vaya a secar esta lluvia.
A menos que me fuese dado
caer ahora para ella, o que me enterrasen
mojado en el agua
que surtiera de todos los fuegos.

¿ Hasta dónde me alcanzará esta lluvia?   10
Temo me quede con algún flanco seco;
temo que ella se vaya, sin haberme probado
en las sequías de increíbles cuerdas vocales,
por las que,
para dar armonía,
hay siempre que subir ¡ nunca bajar!
¿ No subimos acaso para abajo?

Canta, lluvia, en la costa aún sin mar!

POEMAS HUMANOS
(1939)

Va corriendo, andando . . .

Va corriendo, andando, huyendo
de sus pies . . .
Va con dos nubes en su nube,
sentado apócrifo, en la mano insertos
sus tristes paras, sus entonces fúnebres.   5

Corre de todo, andando
entre protestas incoloras; huye
subiendo, huye
bajando, huye
a paso de sotana, huye   10
alzando al mal en brazos,
huye
directamente a sollozar a solas.

Adonde vaya,
lejos de sus fragosos, cáusticos talones,   15
lejos del aire, lejos de su viaje,
a fin de huir, huir y huir y huir
de sus pies—hombre en dos pies, parado
de tanto huir—habrá sed de correr.

¡ Y ni el árbol, si endosa hierro de oro!   20
¡ Y ni el hierro, si cubre su hojarasca!
Nada, sino sus pies,
nada sino su breve calofrío,
sus paras vivos, sus entonces vivos . . .

Un pilar soportando consuelos . . .

Un pilar soportando consuelos,
pilar otro,

125

pilar en duplicado, pilaroso
y como nieto de una puerta oscura.
5   Ruido perdido, el uno, oyendo, al borde del cansancio;
bebiendo, el otro, dos a dos, con asas.

¿ Ignoro acaso el año de este día,
el odio de este amor, las tablas de esta frente?
¿ Ignoro que esta tarde cuesta días?
10 ¿ Ignoro que jamás se dice "nunca", de rodillas?

Los pilares que vi me están oyendo;
otros pilares son, doses y nietos tristes de mi pierna.
¡ Lo digo en cobre americano,
que le bebe a la plata tanto fuego!

15 Consolado en terceras nupcias,
pálido, nacido,
voy a cerrar mi pila bautismal, esta vidriera,
este susto con tetas,
este dedo en capilla,
20 corazónmente unido a mi esqueleto.

Epístola a los transeúntes

Reanudo mi día de conejo,
mi noche de elefante en descanso.

Y, entre mí, digo:
ésta es mi inmensidad en bruto, a cántaros,
5   éste es mi grato peso, que me buscara abajo para pájaro;
éste es mi brazo
que por su cuenta rehusó ser ala;
éstas son mis sagradas escrituras,
éstos mis alarmados compañones.

Lúgubre isla me alumbrará continental,   10
mientras el capitolio se apoye en mi íntimo derrumbe
y la asamblea en lanzas clausure mi desfile.

Pero cuando yo muera
de vida y no de tiempo,
cuando lleguen a dos mis dos maletas,   15
éste ha de ser mi estómago en que cupo mi lámpara en pedazos,
ésta aquella cabeza que expió los tormentos del
                              círculo en mis pasos,
éstos esos gusanos que el corazón contó por unidades,
éste ha de ser mi cuerpo solidario
por el que vela el alma individual; éste ha de ser   20
mi ombligo en que maté mis piojos natos,
ésta mi cosa cosa, mi cosa tremebunda.

En tanto, convulsiva, ásperamente
convalece mi freno,
sufriendo como sufro del lenguaje directo del león;   25
y, puesto que he existido entre dos potestades de ladrillo,
convalezco yo mismo sonriendo de mis labios.

Quiere y no quiere . . .

Quiere y no quiere su color mi pecho,
por cuyas bruscas vías voy, lloro con palo,
trato de ser feliz, lloro en mi mano,
recuerdo, escribo
y remacho una lágrima en mi pómulo.   5

Quiere su rojo el mal, el bien su rojo enrojecido
por el hacha suspensa,
por el trote del ala a pie volando,
y no quiere y sensiblemente
no quiere aquesto el hombre;   10

no quiere estar en su alma
acostado, en la sien latidos de asta,
el bimano, el muy bruto, el muy filósofo.

Así, casi no soy, me vengo abajo
15 desde el arado en que socorro a mi alma
y casi, en proporción, casi enaltézcome.
Que saber por qué tiene la vida este perrazo,
por qué lloro, por qué,
cejón, inhábil, veleidoso, hube nacido
20 gritando;
saberlo, comprenderlo
al son de un alfabeto competente,
sería padecer por un ingrato.

¡ Y no! ¡ No! ¡ No! ¡ Qué ardid, ni paramento!
25 Congoja, sí, con sí firme y frenético,
coriáceo, rapaz, quiere y no quiere, cielo y pájaro;
congoja, sí, con toda la bragueta.
Contienda entre dos llantos, robo de una sola ventura,
vía indolora en que padezco en chanclos
30 de la velocidad de andar a ciegas.

Salutación angélica

Eslavo con respecto a la palmera,
alemán de perfil al sol, inglés sin fin,
francés en cita con los caracoles,
italiano ex profeso, escandinavo de aire,
5 español de pura bestia, tal el cielo
ensartado en la tierra por los vientos,
tal el beso del límite en los hombros.

Mas sólo tú demuestras, descendiendo
o subiendo del pecho, bolchevique,
10 tus trazos confundibles,

tu gesto marital,
tu cara de padre,
tus piernas de amado,
tu cutis por teléfono,
tu alma perpendicular   15
a la mía,
tus codos de justo
y un pasaporte en blanco en tu sonrisa.

Obrando por el hombre, en nuestras pausas,
matando, tú, a lo largo de tu muerte   20
y a lo ancho de un abrazo salubérrimo,
vi que cuando comías después, tenías gusto,
vi que en tus sustantivos creció yerba.

Yo quisiera, por eso,
tu calor doctrinal, frío y en barras,   25
tu añadida manera de mirarnos
y aquesos tuyos pasos metalúrgicos,
aquesos tuyos pasos de otra vida.

Y digo, bolchevique, tomando esta flaqueza
en su feroz linaje de exhalación terrestre: 30
hijo natural del bien y del mal
y viviendo talvez por vanidad, para que digan,
me dan tus simultáneas estaturas mucha pena,
puesto que tú no ignoras en quién se me hace
                            tarde diariamente,
en quién estoy callado y medio tuerto.   35

Al fin, un monte . . .

Al fin, un monte
detrás de la bajura; al fin, humeante nimbo
alrededor, durante un rostro fijo.

Monte en honor del pozo,
5   sobre filones de gratuita plata de oro.

Es la franja a que arrástranse,
seguras de sus tonos de verano,
las que eran largas válvulas difuntas;
el taciturno marco de este arranque
10   natural, de este augusto zapatazo,
de esta piel, de este intrínseco destello
digital, en que estoy entero, lúbrico.

Quehaceres en un pie, mecha de azufre,
oro de plata y plata hecha de plata
15   y mi muerte, mi hondura, mi colina.

¡ Pasar
abrazado a mis brazos,
destaparme después o antes del corcho!
Monte que tantas veces manara
20   oración, prosa fluvial de llanas lágrimas;
monte bajo, compuesto de suplicantes gradas
y, más allá, de torrenciales torres;
niebla entre el día y el alcohol del día,
caro verdor de coles, tibios asnos
25   complementarios, palos y maderas;
filones de gratuita plata de oro.

La rueda del hambriento

Por entre mis propios dientes salgo humeando,
dando voces, pujando,
bajándome los pantalones . . .
Vaca mi estómago, vaca mi yeyuno,
5   la miseria me saca por entre mis propios dientes,
cogido con un palito por el puño de la camisa.

Una piedra en que sentarme
¿ no habrá ahora para mí?
Aun aquella piedra en que tropieza la mujer que
                    ha dado a luz,
la madre del cordero, la causa, la raíz,   10
¿ ésa no habrá ahora para mí?
¡ Siquiera aquella otra,
que ha pasado agachándose por mi alma!
Siquiera
la calcárida o la mala (humilde océano)   15
o la que ya no sirve ni para ser tirada contra el hombre,
¡ ésa dádmela ahora para mí!

Siquiera la que hallaren atravesada y sola en un insulto,
¡ ésa dádmela ahora para mí!
Siquiera la torcida y coronada, en que resuena   20
solamente una vez el andar de las rectas conciencias,
o, al menos, esa otra, que arrojada en digna curva,
va a caer por sí misma,
en profesión de entraña verdadera,
¡ ésa dádmela ahora para mí!   25

Un pedazo de pan, ¿ tampoco habrá ahora para mí?
Ya no más he de ser lo que siempre he de ser,
pero dadme
una piedra en que sentarme,
pero dadme,   30
por favor, un pedazo de pan en que sentarme,
pero dadme
en español
algo, en fin, de beber, de comer, de vivir, de reposarse,
y después me iré . . .   35
Hallo una extraña forma, está muy rota
y sucia mi camisa
y ya no tengo nada, esto es horrendo.

Ello es que . . .

Ello es que el lugar donde me pongo
el pantalón, es una casa donde
me quito la camisa en alta voz
y donde tengo un suelo, un alma, un mapa de mi España.
5   Ahora mismo hablaba
de mí conmigo, y ponía
sobre un pequeño libro un pan tremendo
y he, luego, hecho el traslado, he trasladado,
queriendo canturrear un poco, el lado
10 derecho de la vida al lado izquierdo;
más tarde, me he lavado todo, el vientre,
briosa, dignamente;
he dado vuelta a ver lo que se ensucia,
he raspado lo que me lleva tan cerca
15 y he ordenado bien el mapa que
cabeceaba o lloraba, no lo sé.

Mi casa, por desgracia, es una casa,
un suelo por ventura, donde vive
con su inscripción mi cucharita amada,
20 mi querido esqueleto ya sin letras,
la navaja, un cigarro permanente.
De veras, cuando pienso
en lo que es la vida,
no puedo evitar de decírselo a Georgette,
25 a fin de comer algo agradable y salir,
por la tarde, comprar un buen periódico,
guardar un día para cuando no haya,
una noche también, para cuando haya
(así se dice en el Perú—me excuso);
30 del mismo modo, sufro con gran cuidado,
a fin de no gritar o de llorar, ya que los ojos
poseen, independientemente de uno, sus pobrezas,
quiero decir, su oficio, algo
que resbala del alma y cae al alma . . .

Habiendo atravesado   35
quince años; después, quince, y, antes, quince,
uno se siente, en realidad, tontillo,
es natural, por lo demás ¡ qué hacer!
¿ Y qué dejar de hacer, que es lo peor?
Sino vivir, sino llegar   40
a ser lo que es uno entre millones
de panes, entre miles de vinos, entre cientos de bocas,
entre el sol y su rayo que es de luna
y entre la misa, el pan, el vino y mi alma.

Hoy es domingo, y por eso,   45
me viene a la cabeza la idea, al pecho el llanto
y a la garganta, así como un gran bulto.
Hoy es domingo, y esto
tiene muchos siglos; de otra manera,
sería, quizá, lunes, y vendríame al corazón la idea,   50
al seso, el llanto
y a la garganta, una gana espantosa de ahogar
lo que ahora siento,
como un hombre que soy y que he sufrido.

Intensidad y altura

Quiero escribir, pero me sale espuma,
quiero decir muchísimo y me atollo;
no hay cifra hablada que no sea suma,
no hay pirámide escrita, sin cogollo.

Quiero escribir, pero me siento puma;   5
quiero laurearme, pero me encebollo.
No hay voz hablada, que no llegue a bruma,
no hay dios ni hijo de dios, sin desarrollo.

Vámonos, pues, por eso, a comer yerba,
carne de llanto, fruta de gemido,   10
nuestra alma melancólica en conserva.

Vámonos! Vámonos! Estoy herido;
vámonos a beber lo ya bebido,
vámonos, cuervo, a fecundar tu cuerva.

Hasta el día en que vuelva . . .

Hasta el día en que vuelva, de esta piedra
nacerá mi talón definitivo,
con su juego de crímenes, su yedra,
su obstinación dramática, su olivo.

5   Hasta el día en que vuelva, prosiguiendo,
con franca rectitud de cojo amargo,
de pozo en pozo, mi periplo, entiendo
que el hombre ha de ser bueno, sin embargo.

Hasta el día en que vuelva y hasta que ande
10   el animal que soy, entre sus jueces,
nuestro bravo meñique será grande,
digno, infinito dedo entre los dedos.

Los nueve monstruos

Y, desgraciadamente,
el dolor crece en el mundo a cada rato,
crece a treinta minutos por segundo, paso a paso,
y la naturaleza del dolor, es el dolor dos veces
5   y la condición del martirio, carnívora, voraz,
es el dolor dos veces
y la función de la yerba purísima, el dolor
dos veces
y el bien de ser, dolernos doblemente.

10 Jamás, hombres humanos,
hubo tanto dolor en el pecho, en la solapa, en la cartera,
en el vaso, en la carnicería, en la aritmética!
Jamás tanto cariño doloroso,

jamás tan cerca arremetió lo lejos,
jamás el fuego nunca   15
jugó mejor su rol de frío muerto!
Jamás, señor ministro de salud, fue la salud
más mortal
y la migraña extrajo tanta frente de la frente!
Y el mueble tuvo en su cajón, dolor,   20
el corazón, en su cajón, dolor,
la lagartija, en su cajón, dolor.

Crece la desdicha, hermanos hombres,
más pronto que la máquina, a diez máquinas, y crece
con la res de Rousseau, con nuestras barbas;   25
crece el mal por razones que ignoramos
y es una inundación con propios líquidos,
con propio barro y propia nube sólida!
Invierte el sufrimiento posiciones, da función
en que el humor acuoso es vertical   30
al pavimento,
el ojo es visto y esta oreja oída,
y esta oreja da nueve campanadas a la hora
del rayo, y nueve carcajadas
a la hora del trigo, y nueve sones hembras   35
a la hora del llanto, y nueve cánticos
a la hora del hambre, y nueve truenos
y nueve látigos, menos un grito.

El dolor nos agarra, hermanos hombres,
por detrás, de perfil,   40
y nos aloca en los cinemas,
nos clava en los gramófonos,
nos desclava en los lechos, cae perpendicularmente
a nuestros boletos, a nuestras cartas;
y es muy grave sufrir, puede uno orar . . .   45
Pues de resultas
del dolor, hay algunos

que nacen, otros crecen, otros mueren,
y otros que nacen y no mueren, otros
50 que sin haber nacido, mueren, y otros
que no nacen ni mueren (Son los más).
Y también de resultas
del sufrimiento, estoy triste
hasta la cabeza, y más triste hasta el tobillo,
55 de ver al pan, crucificado, al nabo,
ensangrentado,
llorando, a la cebolla,
al cereal, en general, harina,
a la sal, hecha polvo, al agua, huyendo,
60 al vino, un ecce-homo,
tan pálida a la nieve, al sol tan ardio!
¡ Cómo, hermanos humanos,
no deciros que ya no puedo y
ya no puedo con tanto cajón,
65 tanto minuto, tanta
lagartija y tanta
inversión, tanto lejos y tanta sed de sed!
Señor Ministro de Salud: ¿ qué hacer?
¡ Ah! desgraciadamente, hombres humanos,
70 hay, hermanos, muchísimo que hacer.

París, octubre 1936

De todo esto yo soy el único que parte.
De este banco me voy, de mis calzones,
de mi gran situación, de mis acciones,
de mi número hendido parte a parte,
5   de todo esto yo soy el único que parte.

De los Campos Elíseos o al dar vuelta
la extraña callejuela de la Luna,
mi defunción se va, parte mi cuna,

y, rodeada de gente, sola, suelta,
mi semejanza humana dase vuelta   10
y despacha sus sombras una a una.

Y me alejo de todo, porque todo
se queda para hacer la coartada:
mi zapato, su ojal, también su lodo
y hasta el doblez del codo   15
de mi propia camisa abotonada.

Sermón sobre la muerte

Y, en fin, pasando luego al dominio de la muerte,
que actúa en escuadrón, previo corchete,
párrafo y llave, mano grande y diéresis,
¿ a qué el pupitre asirio? ¿ a qué el cristiano púlpito,
el intenso jalón del mueble vándalo   5
o, todavía menos, este esdrújulo retiro?

¿ Es para terminar,
mañana, en prototipo del alarde fálico,
en diabetes y en blanca vacinica,
en rostro geométrico, en difunto,   10
que se hacen menester sermón y almendras,
que sobran literalmente patatas
y este espectro fluvial en que arde el oro
y en que se quema el precio de la nieve?
¿ Es para eso, que morimos tanto?   15
¿ Para sólo morir,
tenemos que morir a cada instante?
¿ Y el párrafo que escribo?
¿ Y el corchete deísta que enarbolo?
¿ Y el escuadrón en que falló mi casco?   20
¿ Y la llave que va a todas las puertas?
¿ Y la forense diéresis, la mano,
mi patata y mi carne y mi contradicción bajo la sábana?

¡ Loco de mí, lobo de mí, cordero
25   de mí, sensato, caballísimo de mí!
¡ Pupitre, sí, toda la vida; púlpito,
también, toda la muerte!
Sermón de la barbarie: estos papeles;
esdrújulo retiro: este pellejo.

30   De esta suerte, cogitabundo, aurífero, brazudo,
defenderé mi presa en dos momentos,
con la voz y también con la laringe,
y del olfato físico con que oro
y del instinto de inmovilidad con que ando,
35   me honraré mientras viva—hay que decirlo;
se enorgullecerán mis moscardones,
porque, al centro, estoy yo, y a la derecha,
también, y a la izquierda, de igual modo.

El acento me pende . . .

El acento me pende del zapato;
le oigo perfectamente
sucumbir, lucir, doblarse en forma de ámbar
y colgar, colorante, mala sombra.
5   Me sobra así el tamaño,
me ven jueces desde un árbol,
me ven con sus espaldas ir de frente,
entrar a mi martillo,
pararme a ver a una niña
10   y, al pie de un urinario, alzar los hombros.

Seguramente nadie está a mi lado,
me importa poco, no lo necesito;
seguramente han dicho que me vaya:
lo siento claramente.

¡ Cruelísimo tamaño el de rezar!   15
¡ Humillación, fulgor, profunda selva!
Me sobra ya tamaño, bruma elástica,
rapidez por encima y desde y junto.
¡ Imperturbable! ¡ Imperturbable! Suenan
luego, después, fatídicos teléfonos.   20
Es el acento: es él.

Considerando en frío ...

Considerando en frío, imparcialmente,
que el hombre es triste, tose y, sin embargo,
se complace en su pecho colorado;
que lo único que hace es componerse
de días;   5
que es lóbrego mamífero y se peina ...

Considerando
que el hombre procede suavemente del trabajo
y repercute jefe, suena subordinado;
que el diagrama del tiempo   10
es constante diorama en sus medallas
y, a medio abrir, sus ojos estudiaron,
desde lejanos tiempos,
su fórmula famélica de masa ...

Comprendiendo sin esfuerzo   15
que el hombre se queda, a veces, pensando,
como queriendo llorar,
y, sujeto a tenderse como objeto,
se hace buen carpintero, suda, mata
y luego canta, almuerza, se abotona ...   20

Considerando también
que el hombre es en verdad un animal
y, no obstante, al voltear, me da con su tristeza
                        en la cabeza ...

Examinando, en fin,
25 sus encontradas piezas, su retrete,
su desesperación, al terminar su día atroz, borrándolo . . .

Comprendiendo
que él sabe que le quiero,
que le odio con afecto y me es, en suma, indiferente . . .

30 Considerando sus documentos generales
y mirando con lentes aquel certificado
que prueba que nació muy pequeñito . . .

le hago una seña,
viene,
35 y le doy un abrazo, emocionado.
¡ Qué más da! Emocionado . . . Emocionado . . .

Traspié entre dos estrellas

¡ Hay gentes tan desgraciadas, que ni siquiera
tienen cuerpo; cuantitativo el pelo,
baja, en pulgadas, la genial pesadumbre;
el modo, arriba;
5 no me busques, la muela del olvido,
parecen salir del aire, sumar suspiros mentalmente, oír
claros azotes en sus paladares!

Vanse de su piel, rascándose el sarcófago en que nacen
y suben por su muerte de hora en hora
10 y caen, a lo largo de su alfabeto gélido, hasta el suelo.

¡ Ay de tanto! ¡ ay de tan poco! ¡ ay de ellas!
¡ Ay en mi cuarto, oyéndolas con lentes!
¡ Ay en mi tórax, cuando compran trajes!
¡ Ay de mi mugre blanca, en su hez mancomunada!

¡ Amadas sean las orejas sánchez,   15
amadas las personas que se sientan,
amado el desconocido y su señora,
el prójimo con mangas, cuello y ojos!

¡ Amado sea aquel que tiene chinches,
el que lleva zapato roto bajo la lluvia,   20
el que vela el cadáver de un pan con dos cerillas,
el que se coge un dedo en una puerta,
el que no tiene cumpleaños,
el que perdió su sombra en un incendio,
el animal, el que parece un loro,   25
el que parece un hombre, el pobre rico,
el puro miserable, el pobre pobre!

¡ Amado sea
el que tiene hambre o sed, pero no tiene
hambre con qué saciar toda su sed,   30
ni sed con qué saciar todas sus hambres!

¡ Amado sea el que trabaja al día, al mes, a la hora,
el que suda de pena o de vergüenza,
aquel que va, por orden de sus manos, al cinema,
el que paga con lo que le falta,   35
el que duerme de espaldas,
el que ya no recuerda su niñez; amado sea
el calvo sin sombrero,
el justo sin espinas,
el ladrón sin rosas,   40
el que lleva reloj y ha visto a Dios,
el que tiene un honor y no fallece!

¡ Amado sea el niño, que cae y aún llora
y el hombre que ha caído y ya no llora!

¡ Ay de tanto! ¡ Ay de tan poco! ¡ Ay de ellos!   45

Hoy le ha entrado una astilla . . .

Hoy le ha entrado una astilla.
Hoy le ha entrado una astilla cerca, dándole
cerca, fuerte, en su modo
de ser y en su centavo ya famoso.
5   Le ha dolido la suerte mucho,
todo;
le ha dolido la puerta,
le ha dolido la faja, dándole
sed, aflixión
10   y sed del vaso pero no del vino.
Hoy le salió a la pobre vecina del aire,
a escondidas, humareda de su dogma;
hoy le ha entrado una astilla.

La inmensidad persíguela
15   a distancia superficial, a un vasto eslabonazo.
Hoy le salió a la pobre vecina del viento,
en la mejilla, norte, y en la mejilla, oriente;
hoy le ha entrado una astilla.

¿ Quién comprará, en los días perecederos, ásperos,
20   un pedacito de café con leche,
y quién, sin ella, bajará a su rastro hasta dar luz?
¿ Quién será, luego, sábado, a las siete?
¡ Tristes son las astillas que le entran
a uno,
25   exactamente ahí precisamente!
Hoy le entró a la pobre vecina de viaje
una llama apagada en el oráculo;
hoy le ha entrado una astilla.

Le ha dolido el dolor, el dolor joven,
30   el dolor niño, el dolorazo, dándole
en las manos

y dándole sed, aflixión
y sed del vaso, pero no del vino.
¡ La pobre pobrecita!

Piedra negra sobre una piedra blanca

Me moriré en París con aguacero,
un día del cual tengo ya el recuerdo.
Me moriré en París—y no me corro—
talvez un jueves, como es hoy, de otoño.

Jueves será, porque hoy, jueves, que proso   5
estos versos, los húmeros me he puesto
a la mala y, jamás como hoy, me he vuelto,
con todo mi camino, a verme solo.

César Vallejo ha muerto, le pegaban
todos sin que él les haga nada;   10
le daban duro con un palo y duro

también con una soga; son testigos
los días jueves y los huesos húmeros,
la soledad, la lluvia, los caminos . . .

Al revés de las aves . . .

Al revés de las aves del monte,
que viven del valle,
aquí, una tarde,
aquí, presa, metaloso, terminante,
vino el Sincero con sus nietos pérfidos,   5
y nosotros quedámonos, que no hay
más madera en la cruz de la derecha,
ni más hierro en el clavo de la izquierda,
que un apretón de manos entre zurdos.

10   Vino el Sincero, ciego, con sus lámparas.
Se vio al Pálido, aquí, bastar
al Encarnado;
nació de puro humilde el Grande;
la guerra,
15   esta tórtola mía, nunca nuestra,
diseñóse, borróse, ovó, matáronla.

Llevóse el Ebrio al labio un roble, porque
amaba, y una astilla
de roble, porque odiaba;
20   trenzáronse las trenzas de los potros
y la crin de las potencias;
cantaron los obreros; fui dichoso.

El Pálido abrazóse al Encarnado
y el Ebrio saludónos, escondiéndose.
25   Como era aquí y al terminar el día,
¡ qué más tiempo que aquella plazoleta!
¡ qué año mejor que esa gente!
¡ qué momento más fuerte que ese siglo!

Pues de lo que hablo no es
30   sino de lo que pasa en esta época, y
de lo que ocurre en China y en España, y en el mundo.
(Walt Whitman tenía un pecho suavísimo y respiraba
y nadie sabe lo que él hacía cuando lloraba en su comedor.)

Pero, volviendo a lo nuestro,
35   y al verso que decía, fuera entonces
que vi que el hombre es malnacido,
mal vivo, mal muerto, mal moribundo,
y, naturalmente,
el tartufo sincero desespérase,
40   el pálido (es el pálido de siempre)

será pálido por algo,
y el ebrio, entre la sangre humana y la leche animal,
abátese, da, y opta por marcharse.

Todo esto
agítase, ahora mismo,   45
en mi vientre de macho extrañamente.

El alma que sufrió de ser su cuerpo

Tú sufres de una glándula endocrínica, se ve,
o, quizá,
sufres de mí, de mi sagacidad escueta, tácita.
Tú padeces del diáfano antropoide, allá, cerca,
donde está la tiniebla tenebrosa.   5
Tú das vuelta al sol, agarrándote el alma,
extendiendo tus juanes corporales
y ajustándote el cuello; eso se ve.
Tú sabes lo que te duele,
lo que te salta al anca,   10
lo que baja por ti con soga al suelo.
Tú, pobre hombre, vives; no lo niegues,
si mueres; no lo niegues,
si mueres de tu edad ¡ ay! y de tu época.
Y, aunque llores, bebes,   15
y, aunque sangres, alimentas a tu híbrido colmillo,
a tu vela tristona y a tus partes.
Tú sufres, tú padeces y tú vuelves a sufrir horriblemente,
desgraciado mono,
jovencito de Darwin,   20
alguacil que me atisbas, atrocísimo microbio.
Y tú lo sabes a tal punto,
que lo ignoras, soltándote a llorar.
Tú, luego, has nacido; eso
también se ve de lejos, infeliz y cállate,   25
y soportas la calle que te dio la suerte
y a tu ombligo interrogas: ¿ dónde? ¿ cómo?

    Amigo mío, estás completamente,
    hasta el pelo, en el año treinta y ocho,
30 nicolás o santiago, tal o cual,
    estés contigo o con tu aborto o con-
    migo,
    y cautivo en tu enorme libertad,
    arrastrado por tu hércules autónomo . . .
35 Pero si tú calculas en tus dedos hasta dos,
    es peor; no lo niegues, hermanito.

      ¿ Que no ? ¿ Que sí, pero que no ?
    ¡ Pobre mono ! . . . ¡ Dame la pata ! . . . No. La mano,
                                he dicho.

    ¡ Salud ! ¡ Y sufre !

Un hombre pasa . . .

Un hombre pasa con un pan al hombro
¿ Voy a escribir, después, sobre mi doble ?

Otro se sienta, ráscase, extrae un piojo de su axila, mátalo
¿ Con qué valor hablar del psicoanálisis ?

5 Otro ha entrado a mi pecho con un palo en la mano
¿ Hablar luego de Sócrates al médico ?

Un cojo pasa dando el brazo a un niño
¿ Voy, después, a leer a André Breton ?

Otro tiembla de frío, tose, escupe sangre
10 ¿ Cabrá aludir jamás al Yo profundo ?

Otro busca en el fango huesos, cáscaras
¿ Cómo escribir, después, del infinito ?

Un albañil cae de un techo, muere, y ya no almuerza
¿ Innovar, luego, el tropo, la metáfora ?

Un comerciante roba un gramo en el peso a un cliente   15
¿Hablar, después, de cuarta dimensión?

Un banquero falsea su balance
¿Con qué cara llorar en el teatro?

Un paria duerme con el pie a la espalda
¿Hablar, después, a nadie de Picasso?   20

Alguien va en un entierro sollozando
¿Cómo luego ingresar a la Academia?

Alguien limpia un fusil en su cocina
¿Con qué valor hablar del más allá?

Alguien pasa contando con sus dedos   25
¿Cómo hablar del no-yo sin dar un grito?

Acaba de pasar ...

Acaba de pasar el que vendrá
proscrito, a sentarse en mi triple desarrollo;
acaba de pasar criminalmente.

Acaba de sentarse más acá,
a un cuerpo de distancia de mi alma,   5
el que vino en un asno a enflaquecerme;
acaba de sentarse de pie, lívido.

Acaba de darme lo que está acabado,
el calor del fuego y el pronombre inmenso
que el animal crió bajo su cola.   10

Acaba
de expresarme su duda sobre hipótesis lejanas
que él aleja, aún más, con la mirada.

Acaba de hacer al bien los honores que le tocan
15   en virtud del infame paquidermo,
por lo soñado en mí y en él matado.

Acaba de ponerme (no hay primera)
su segunda aflixión en plenos lomos
y su tercer sudor en plena lágrima.

20   Acaba de pasar sin haber venido.

Palmas y guitarra

Ahora, entre nosotros, aquí,
ven conmigo, trae por la mano a tu cuerpo
y cenemos juntos y pasemos un instante la vida
a dos vidas y dando una parte a nuestra muerte.
5   Ahora, ven contigo, hazme el favor
de quejarte en mi nombre y a la luz de la noche teneblosa
en que traes a tu alma de la mano
y huimos en puntillas de nosotros.

Ven a mí, sí, y a ti, sí,
10   con paso par, a vernos a los dos con paso impar,
marcar el paso de la despedida.
¡ Hasta cuando volvamos! ¡ Hasta la vuelta!
¡ Hasta cuando leamos, ignorantes!
¡ Hasta cuando volvamos, despidámonos!

15   ¿ Qué me importan los fusiles,
escúchame;
escúchame, qué impórtanme,
si la bala circula ya en el rango de mi firma?
¿ Qué te importan a ti las balas,
20   si el fusil está humeando ya en tu olor?
Hoy mismo pesaremos
en los brazos de un ciego nuestra estrella
y, una vez que me cantes, lloraremos.

Hoy mismo, hermosa, con tu paso par
y tu confianza a que llegó mi alarma,   25
saldremos de nosotros, dos a dos.
¡ Hasta cuando seamos ciegos!
¡ Hasta
que lloremos de tanto volver!

Ahora,   30
entre nosotros, trae
por la mano a tu dulce personaje
y cenemos juntos y pasemos un instante la vida
a dos vidas y dando una parte a nuestra muerte.
Ahora, ven contigo, hazme el favor   35
de cantar algo
y de tocar en tu alma, haciendo palmas.
¡ Hasta cuando volvamos! ¡ Hasta entonces!
¡ Hasta cuando partamos, despidámonos!

Me viene, hay días . . .

   Me viene, hay días, una gana ubérrima, política,
de querer, de besar al cariño en sus dos rostros,
y me viene de lejos un querer
demostrativo, otro querer amar, de grado o fuerza,
al que me odia, al que rasga su papel, al muchachito,   5
a la que llora por el que lloraba,
al rey del vino, al esclavo del agua,
al que ocultóse en su ira,
al que suda, al que pasa, al que sacude su persona en mi
                                                      alma.
Y quiero, por lo tanto, acomodarle   10
al que me habla, su trenza; sus cabellos, al soldado;
su luz, al grande; su grandeza, al chico.
Quiero planchar directamente
un pañuelo al que no puede llorar
y, cuando estoy triste o me duele la dicha,   15
remendar a los niños y a los genios.

Quiero ayudar al bueno a ser su poquillo de malo
y me urge estar sentado
a la diestra del zurdo, y responder al mudo,
20   tratando de serle útil en
lo que puedo, y también quiero muchísimo
lavarle al cojo el pie
y ayudarle a dormir al tuerto próximo.

¡ Ah querer, éste, el mío, éste, el mundial,
25   interhumano y parroquial, provecto!
Me viene a pelo,
desde el cimiento, desde la ingle pública,
y, viniendo de lejos, da ganas de besarle
la bufanda al cantor,
30   y al que sufre, besarle en su sartén,
al sordo, en su rumor craneano, impávido;
al que me da lo que olvidé en mi seno,
en su Dante, en su Chaplin, en sus hombros.

Quiero, para terminar,
35   cuando estoy al borde célebre de la violencia,
o lleno de pecho el corazón, querría
ayudar a reír al que sonríe,
ponerle un pajarillo al malvado en plena nuca,
cuidar a los enfermos enfadándolos,
40   comprarle al vendedor,
ayudarle a matar al matador — cosa terrible —
y quisiera yo ser bueno conmigo
en todo.

Los desgraciados

Ya va a venir el día; da
cuerda a tu brazo, búscate debajo
del colchón, vuelve a pararte
en tu cabeza, para andar derecho.
5   Ya va a venir el día, ponte el saco.

Ya va a venir el día; ten
fuerte en la mano a tu intestino grande, reflexiona,
antes de meditar, pues es horrible
cuando le cae a uno la desgracia
y se le cae a uno a fondo el diente.   10

Necesitas comer, pero, me digo,
no tengas pena, que no es de pobres
la pena, el sollozar junto a su tumba;
remiéndate, recuerda,
confía en tu hilo blanco, fuma, pasa lista   15
a tu cadena y guárdala detrás de tu retrato.
Ya va a venir el día, ponte el alma.

Ya va a venir el día; pasan,
han abierto en el hotel un ojo,
azotándolo, dándole con un espejo tuyo . . .   20
¿Tiemblas? Es el estado remoto de la frente
y la nación reciente del estómago.
Roncan aún! . . . ¡Qué universo se lleva este ronquido!
¡Cómo quedan tus poros, enjuiciándolo!
¡Con cuántos doses, ¡ay! estás tan solo!   25
Ya va a venir el día, ponte el sueño.

Ya va a venir el día, repito
por el órgano oral de tu silencio
y urge tomar la izquierda con el hambre
y tomar la derecha con la sed; de todos modos,   30
absténte de ser pobre con los ricos,
atiza
tu frío, porque en él se integra mi calor, amada víctima.
Ya va a venir el día, ponte el cuerpo.

Ya va a venir el día;   35
la mañana, la mar, el meteoro, van
en pos de tu cansancio, con banderas,

y, por tu orgullo clásico, las hienas
cuentan sus pasos al compás del asno,
40 la panadera piensa en ti,
el carnicero piensa en ti, palpando
el hacha en que están presos
el acero y el hierro y el metal; jamás olvides
que durante la misa no hay amigos.
45 Ya va a venir el día, ponte el sol.

Ya viene el día; dobla
el aliento, triplica
tu bondad rencorosa
y da codos al miedo, nexo y énfasis,
50 pues tú, como se observa en tu entrepierna y siendo
el malo ¡ ay! inmortal,
has soñado esta noche que vivías
de nada y morías de todo . . .

Parado en una piedra . . .

Parado en una piedra,
desocupado,
astroso, espeluznante,
a la orilla del Sena, va y viene.
5   Del río brota entonces la conciencia,
con peciolo y rasguños de árbol ávido:
del río sube y baja la ciudad, hecha de lobos abrazados.

El parado la ve yendo y viniendo,
monumental, llevando sus ayunos en la cabeza cóncava,
10 en el pecho sus piojos purísimos
y abajo
su pequeño sonido, el de su pelvis,
callado entre dos grandes decisiones,
y abajo,
15 más abajo,
un papelito, un clavo, una cerilla . . .

¡ Éste es, trabajadores, aquel
que en la labor sudaba para afuera,
que suda hoy para adentro su secreción de sangre rehusada !
Fundidor del cañón, que sabe cuántas zarpas son acero,   20
tejedor que conoce los hilos positivos de sus venas,
albañil de pirámides,
constructor de descensos por columnas
serenas, por fracasos triunfales,
parado individual entre treinta millones de parados,   25
andante en multitud,
¡ qué salto el retratado en su talón
y qué humo el de su boca ayuna, y cómo
su talle incide, canto a canto, en su herramienta atroz, parada,
y qué idea de dolorosa válvula en su pómulo !   30

También parado el hierro frente al horno,
paradas las semillas con sus sumisas síntesis al aire,
parados los petróleos conexos,
parada en sus auténticos apóstrofes la luz,
parados de crecer los laureles,   35
paradas en un pie las aguas móviles
y hasta la tierra misma, parada de estupor ante este paro,
¡ qué salto el retratado en sus tendones !
¡ qué transmisión entablan sus cien pasos !
¡ cómo chilla el motor en su tobillo !   40
¡ cómo gruñe el reloj, paseándose impaciente a sus espaldas !
¡ cómo oye deglutir a los patrones
el trago que le falta, camaradas,
y el pan que se equivoca de saliva,
y, oyéndolo, sintiéndolo, en plural, humanamente,   45
cómo clava el relámpago
su fuerza sin cabeza en su cabeza !
y lo que hacen, abajo, entonces, ¡ ay !
más abajo, camaradas,
el papelucho, el clavo, la cerilla,   50
el pequeño sonido, el piojo padre !

Altura y pelos

¿ Quién no tiene su vestido azul?
¿ Quién no almuerza y no toma el tranvía,
con su cigarrillo contratado y su dolor de bolsillo?
¡ Yo que tan sólo he nacido!
5   ¡ Yo que tan sólo he nacido!

¿ Quién no escribe una carta?
¿ Quién no habla de un asunto muy importante,
muriendo de costumbre y llorando de oído?
¡ Yo que solamente he nacido!
10   ¡ Yo que solamente he nacido!

¿ Quién no se llama Carlos o cualquier otra cosa?
¿ Quién al gato no dice gato gato?
¡ Ay, yo que sólo he nacido solamente!
¡ Ay, yo que sólo he nacido solamente!

¿ Qué me da . . . ?

¿ Qué me da, que me azoto con la línea
y creo que me sigue, al trote, el punto?

¿ Qué me da, que me he puesto
en los hombros un huevo en vez de un manto?

5   ¿ Qué me ha dado, que vivo?
¿ Qué me ha dado, que muero?

¿ Qué me da, que tengo ojos?
¿ Qué me da, que tengo alma?

¿ Qué me da, que se acaba en mí mi prójimo
10   y empieza en mi carrillo el rol del viento?

¿ Qué me ha dado, que cuento mis dos lágrimas,
sollozo tierra y cuelgo el horizonte?

¿ Qué me ha dado, que lloro de no poder llorar
y río de lo poco que he reído?

¿ Qué me da, que ni vivo ni muero?   15

Oye a tu masa . . .

Oye a tu masa, a tu cometa, escúchalos; no gimas
de memoria, gravísimo cetáceo;
oye a la túnica en que estás dormido,
oye a tu desnudez, dueña del sueño.

Relátate agarrándote   5
de la cola del fuego y a los cuernos
en que acaba la crin su atroz carrera;
rómpete, pero en círculos;
fórmate, pero en columnas combas;
descríbete atmosférico, ser de humo,   10
a paso redoblado de esqueleto.

¿ La muerte? ¡ Opónle todo tu vestido!
¿ La vida? ¡ Opónle parte de tu muerte!
Bestia dichosa, piensa;
dios desgraciado, quítate la frente.   15
Luego, hablaremos.

¡ Y si después de tantas palabras . . . !

¡ Y si después de tantas palabras,
no sobrevive la palabra!
¡ Si después de las alas de los pájaros,
no sobrevive el pájaro parado!
¡ Más valdría, en verdad,   5
que se lo coman todo y acabemos!

¡ Haber nacido para vivir de nuestra muerte!
¡ Levantarse del cielo hacia la tierra
por sus propios desastres
10 y espiar el momento de apagar con su sombra su tiniebla!
¡ Más valdría, francamente,
que se lo coman todo y qué más da!...

¡ Y si después de tanta historia, sucumbimos,
no ya de eternidad,
15 sino de esas cosas sencillas, como estar
en la casa o ponerse a cavilar!
¡ Y si luego encontramos,
de buenas a primeras, que vivimos,
a juzgar por la altura de los astros,
20 por el peine y las manchas del pañuelo!
¡ Más valdría, en verdad,
que se lo coman todo, desde luego!

Se dirá que tenemos
en uno de los ojos mucha pena
25 y también en el otro, mucha pena
y en los dos, cuando miran, mucha pena...
Entonces... ¡ Claro !... Entonces... ¡ ni palabra!

Marcha nupcial

A la cabeza de mis propios actos,
corona en mano, batallón de dioses,
el signo negativo al cuello, atroces
el fósforo y la prisa, estupefactos
5 el alma y el valor, con dos impactos

al pie de la mirada; dando voces;
los límites, dinámicos, feroces;
tragándome los lloros inexactos,

me encenderé, se encenderá mi hormiga,
se encenderán mi llave, la querella   10
en que perdí la causa de mi huella.

Luego, haciendo del átomo una espiga,
encenderé mis hoces al pie de ella
y la espiga será por fin espiga.

Nómina de huesos

Se pedía a grandes voces:
— Que muestre las dos manos a la vez.
Y esto no fue posible.
— Que, mientras llora, le tomen la medida de sus pasos.
Y esto no fue posible.   5
— Que piense un pensamiento idéntico, en el tiempo en que
un cero permanece inútil.
Y esto no fue posible.
— Que haga una locura.
Y esto no fue posible.   10
— Que entre él y otro hombre semejante a él, se interponga
una muchedumbre de hombres como él.
Y esto no fue posible.
— Que le comparen consigo mismo.
Y esto no fue posible.   15
— Que le llamen, en fin, por su nombre.
Y esto no fue posible.

Existe un mutilado . . .

Existe un mutilado, no de un combate sino de un abrazo, no
de la guerra sino de la paz. Perdió el rostro en el amor y no
en el odio. Lo perdió en el curso normal de la vida y no en
un accidente. Lo perdió en el orden de la naturaleza y no
en el desorden de los hombres. El coronel Piccot, Presidente   5
de "Les gueules cassées", lleva la boca comida por la

pólvora de 1914. Este mutilado que conozco, lleva el rostro comido por el aire inmortal e inmemorial.

Rostro muerto sobre el tronco vivo. Rostro yerto y pegado
10 con clavos a la cabeza viva. Este rostro resulta ser el dorso del cráneo, el cráneo del cráneo. Vi una vez un árbol darme la espalda y vi otra vez un camino que me daba la espalda. Un árbol de espaldas sólo crece en los lugares donde nunca nació ni murió nadie. Un camino de espaldas sólo avanza
15 por los lugares donde ha habido todas las muertes y ningún nacimiento. El mutilado de la paz y del amor, del abrazo y del orden y que lleva el rostro muerto sobre el tronco vivo, nació a la sombra de un árbol de espaldas y su existencia trascurre a lo largo de un camino de espaldas.
20   Como el rostro está yerto y difunto, toda la vida psíquica, toda la expresión animal de este hombre, se refugia, para traducirse al exterior, en el peludo cráneo, en el tórax y en las extremidades. Los impulsos de su ser profundo, al salir, retroceden del rostro y la respiración, el olfato, la vista, el
25 oído, la palabra, el resplandor humano de su ser, funcionan y se expresan por el pecho, por los hombros, por el cabello, por las costillas, por los brazos y las piernas y los pies.

Mutilado del rostro, tapado del rostro, cerrado del rostro,
30 este hombre, no obstante, está entero y nada le hace falta. No tiene ojos y ve y llora. No tiene narices y huele y respira. No tiene oídos y escucha. No tiene boca y habla y sonríe. No tiene frente y piensa y se sume en sí mismo. No tiene mentón y quiere y subsiste. Jesús conocía al mutilado
35 de la función, que tenía ojos y no veía y tenía orejas y no oía. Yo conozco al mutilado del órgano, que ve sin ojos y oye sin orejas.

Voy a hablar de la esperanza

Yo no sufro este dolor como César Vallejo. Yo no me duelo ahora como artista, como hombre ni como simple

ser vivo siquiera. Yo no sufro este dolor como católico,
como mahometano ni como ateo. Hoy sufro solamente. Si
no me llamase César Vallejo, también sufriría este mismo   5
dolor. Si no fuese artista, también lo sufriría. Si no fuese
hombre ni ser vivo siquiera, también lo sufriría. Si no fuese
católico, ateo ni mahometano, también lo sufriría. Hoy sufro
desde más abajo. Hoy sufro solamente.

Me duelo ahora sin explicaciones. Mi dolor es tan hondo,   10
que no tuvo ya causa ni carece de causa. ¿ Qué sería su
causa? ¿ Dónde está aquello tan importante, que dejase de
ser su causa? Nada es su causa; nada ha podido dejar de
ser su causa. ¿ A qué ha nacido este dolor, por sí mismo?
Mi dolor es del viento del norte y del viento del sur, como   15
esos huevos neutros que algunas aves raras ponend el viento.
Si hubiera muerto mi novia, mi dolor sería igual. Si me
hubieran cortado el cuello de raíz, mi dolor sería igual. Si
la vida fuese, en fin, de otro modo, mi dolor sería igual.
Hoy sufro desde más arriba. Hoy sufro solamente.   20

Miro el dolor del hambriento y veo que su hambre anda
tan lejos de mi sufrimiento, que de quedarme ayuno hasta
morir, saldría siempre de mi tumba una brizna de yerba
al menos. Lo mismo el enamorado. ¡ Qué sangre la suya
más engendrada, para la mía sin fuente ni consumo!   25

Yo creía hasta ahora que todas las cosas del universo
eran, inevitablemente, padres o hijos. Pero he aquí que mi
dolor de hoy no es padre ni es hijo. Le falta espalda para
anochecer, tanto como le sobra pecho para amanecer y si lo
pusiesen en una estancia oscura, no daría luz y si lo pus-   30
iesen en una estancia luminosa, no echaría sombra. Hoy
sufro suceda lo que suceda. Hoy sufro solamente.

ESPAÑA, APARTA DE MÍ ESTE CÁLIZ
(1939)

Himno a los voluntarios de la República

Voluntario de España, miliciano
de huesos fidedignos, cuando marcha a morir tu corazón,
cuando marcha a matar con su agonía
mundial, no sé verdaderamente
qué hacer, dónde ponerme; corro, escribo, aplaudo,   5
lloro, atisbo, destrozo, apagan, digo
a mi pecho que acabe, al bien, que venga,
y quiero desgraciarme;
descúbrome la frente impersonal hasta tocar
el vaso de la sangre, me detengo,   10
detienen mi tamaño esas famosas caídas de arquitecto
con las que se honra el animal que me honra;
refluyen mis instintos a sus sogas,
humea ante mi tumba la alegría
y, otra vez, sin saber qué hacer, sin nada, déjame,   15
desde mi piedra en blanco, déjame,
solo,
cuadrumano, más acá, mucho más lejos,
al no caber entre mis manos tu largo rato extático,
quiebro contra tu rapidez de doble filo   20
mi pequeñez en traje de grandeza!

Un día diurno, claro, atento, fértil
¡ oh bienio, el de los lóbregos semestres suplicantes,
por el que iba la pólvora mordiéndose los codos!
¡ oh dura pena y más duros pedernales!   25
¡ oh frenos los tascados por el pueblo!
Un día prendió el pueblo su fósforo cautivo, oró de cólera
y soberanamente pleno, circular,
cerró su natalicio con manos electivas;
arrastraban candado ya los déspotas   30
y en el candado, sus bacterias muertas . . .

161

¿Batallas? ¡No! ¡Pasiones! Y pasiones precedidas
de dolores con rejas de esperanzas,
¡de dolores de pueblo con esperanzas de hombres!
35   ¡Muerte y pasión de paz, las populares!
¡Muerte y pasión guerreras entre olivos, entendámonos!
Tal en tu aliento cambian de agujas atmosféricas los vientos
y de llave las tumbas en tu pecho,
tu frontal elevándose a primera potencia de martirio.

40   El mundo exclama: "¡Cosas de españoles!" Y es
                                    verdad. Consideremos,
durante una balanza, a quema ropa,
a Calderón, dormido sobre la cola de un anfibio muerto,
o a Cervantes, diciendo: "Mi reino es de este mundo, pero
también del otro": ¡punta y filo en dos papeles!
45   Contemplemos a Goya, de hinojos y rezando ante un espejo,
a Coll, el paladín en cuyo asalto cartesiano
tuvo un sudor de nube el paso llano,
o a Quevedo, ese abuelo instantáneo de los dinamiteros,
o a Cajal, devorado por su pequeño infinito, o todavía
50   a Teresa, mujer, que muere porque no muere,
o a Lina Odena, en pugna en más de un punto con Teresa . . .
(Todo acto o voz genial viene del pueblo
y va hacia él, de frente o transmitido
por incesantes briznas, por el humo rosado
55   de amargas contraseñas sin fortuna.)
Así tu criatura, miliciano, así tu exangüe criatura,
agitada por una piedra inmóvil,
se sacrifica, apártase,
decae para arriba y por su llama incombustible sube,
60   sube hasta los débiles,
distribuyendo españas a los toros,
toros a las palomas . . .

Proletario que mueres de universo, ¡en qué frenética armonía
acabará tu grandeza, tu miseria, tu vorágine impelente,
tu violencia metódica, tu caos teórico y práctico, tu gana   65
dantesca, españolísima, de amar, aunque sea a traición,
                                                a tu enemigo!
¡ Liberador ceñido de grilletes,
sin cuyo esfuerzo hasta hoy continuaría sin asas la extensión,
vagarían acéfalos los clavos,
antiguo, lento, colorado, el día,   70
nuestros amados cascos, insepultos!
¡ Campesino caído con tu verde follaje por el hombre,
con la inflexión social de tu meñique,
con tu buey que se queda, con tu física,
también con tu palabra atada a un palo   75
y tu cielo arrendado
y con la arcilla inserta en tu cansancio
y la que estaba en tu uña, caminando!
¡ Constructores
agrícolas, civiles y guerreros,   80
de la activa, hormigueante eternidad: estaba escrito
que vosotros haríais la luz, entornando
con la muerte vuestros ojos;
que, a la caída cruel de vuestras bocas,
vendrá en siete bandejas la abundancia, todo   85
en el mundo será de oro súbito
y el oro,
fabulosos mendigos de vuestra propia secreción de sangre,
y el oro mismo será entonces de oro!

¡ Se amarán todos los hombres   90
y comerán tomados de las puntas de vuestros pañuelos tristes
y beberán en nombre
de vusetras gargantas infaustas!
Descansarán andando al pie de esta carrera,
sollozarán pensando en vuestras órbitas, venturosos   95
serán y al son

de vuestro atroz retorno, florecido, innato,
ajustarán mañana sus quehaceres, sus figuras soñadas y
cantadas!

    ¡ Unos mismos zapatos irán bien al que asciende
100   sin vías a su cuerpo
y al que baja hasta la forma de su alma!
¡ Entrelazándose hablarán los mudos, los tullidos andarán!
¡ Verán, ya de regreso, los ciegos
y palpitando escucharán los sordos!
105   ¡ Sabrán los ignorantes, ignorarán los sabios!
¡ Serán dados los besos que no pudisteis dar!
¡ Sólo la muerte morirá! ¡ La hormiga
traerá pedacitos de pan al elefante encadenado
a su brutal delicadeza; volverán
110   los niños abortados a nacer perfectos, espaciales
y trabajarán todos los hombres,
engendrarán todos los hombres,
comprenderán todos los hombres!

    ¡ Obrero, salvador, redentor nuestro,
115   perdónanos, hermano, nuestras deudas!
Como dice un tambor al redoblar, en sus adagios:
¡ qué jamás tan efímero, tu espalda!
¡ qué siempre tan cambiante, tu perfil!

    ¡ Voluntario italiano, entre cuyos animales de batalla
120   un león abisinio va cojeando!
¡ Voluntario soviético, marchando a la cabeza de tu pecho

    ¡ Voluntarios del sur, del norte, del oriente
y tú, el occidental, cerrando el canto fúnebre del alba!
¡ Soldado conocido, cuyo nombre
125   desfila en el sonido de un abrazo!

¡ Combatiente que la tierra criara, armándote
de polvo,
calzándote de imanes positivos,
vigentes tus creencias personales,
distinto de carácter, íntima tu férula,   130
el cutis inmediato,
andándote tu idioma por los hombros
y el alma coronada de guijarros!
¡ Voluntario fajado de tu zona fría,
templada o tórrida,   135
héroes a la redonda,
víctima en columna de vencedores:
en España, en Madrid, están llamando
a matar, voluntarios de la vida!

Porque en España matan, otros matan   140
al niño, a su juguete que se para,
a la madre Rosenda esplendorosa,
al viejo Adán que hablaba en alta voz con su caballo
y al perro que dormía en la escalera.
¡ Matan al libro, tiran a sus verbos auxiliares, 145
a su indefensa página primera!
Matan el caso exacto de la estatua,
al sabio, a su bastón, a su colega,
al barbero de al lado — me cortó posiblemente,
pero buen hombre y, luego, infortunado;   150
al mendigo que ayer cantaba enfrente,
a la enfermera que hoy pasó llorando,
al sacerdote a cuestas con la altura tenaz de sus rodillas . . .

¡ Voluntarios,
por la vida, por los buenos, matad   155
a la muerte, matad a los malos!
¡ Hacedlo por la libertad de todos,
del explotado y del explotador,

por la paz indolora — la sospecho
160 cuando duermo al pie de mi frente
y más cuando circulo dando voces —
y hacedlo, voy diciendo,
por el analfabeto a quien escribo,
por el genio descalzo y su cordero,
165 por los camaradas caídos,
sus cenizas abrazadas al cadáver de un camino!

Para que vosotros,
voluntarios de España y del mundo, vinierais,
soñé que era yo bueno, y era para ver
170 vuestra sangre, voluntarios . . .
De esto hace mucho pecho, muchas ansias,
muchos camellos en edad de orar.
Marcha hoy de vuestra parte el bien ardiendo,
os siguen con cariño los reptiles de pestaña inmanente
175 y, a dos pasos, a uno,
la dirección del agua que corre a ver su límite antes que
arda.

Los mendigos . . .

Los mendigos pelean por España,
mendigando en París, en Roma, en Praga
y refrendando así, con mano gótica, rogante,
los pies de los Apóstoles, en Londres, en New York, en
Méjico.
5 Los pordioseros luchan suplicando infernalmente
a Dios por Santander,
la lid en que ya nadie es derrotado.
Al sufrimiento antiguo
danse, encarnízanse en llorar plomo social
10 al pie del individuo,
y atacan a gemidos, los mendigos,
matando con tan sólo ser mendigos.

Ruegos de infantería,
en que el arma ruega del metal para arriba,
y ruega la ira, más acá de la pólvora iracunda.   15
Tácitos escuadrones que disparan,
con cadencia mortal, su mansedumbre,
desde un umbral, desde sí mismos, ¡ ay! desde sí mismos.
Potenciales guerreros
sin calcetines al calzar el trueno,   20
satánicos, numéricos,
arrastrando sus títulos de fuerza,
migaja al cinto,
fusil doble calibre: sangre y sangre.
¡ El poeta saluda al sufrimiento armado!   25

Masa

Al fin de la batalla,
y muerto el combatiente, vino hacia él un hombre
y le dijo: "¡ No mueras; te amo tanto!"
Pero el cadáver ¡ ay! siguió muriendo.

Se le acercaron dos y repitiéronle: 5
"¡ No nos dejes! ¡ Valor! ¡ Vuelve a la vida!"
Pero el cadáver ¡ ay! siguió muriendo.

Acudieron a él veinte, cien, mil, quinientos mil,
clamando: "¡ Tanto amor, y no poder nada contra la muerte!"
Pero el cadáver ¡ ay!, siguió muriendo.   10

Le rodearon millones de individuos,
con un ruego común: "¡ Quédate, hermano!"
Pero el cadáver ¡ ay! siguió muriendo.

Entonces, todos los hombres de la tierra
le rodearon; les vio el cadáver triste, emocionado;   15
incorporóse lentamente,
abrazó al primer hombre; echóse a andar . . .

España, aparta de mí este cáliz

Niños del mundo,
si cae España — digo, es un decir —
si cae
del cielo abajo su antebrazo que asen,
5   en cabestro, dos láminas terrestres;
niños, ¡ qué edad la de las sienes cóncavas!
¡ qué temprano en el sol lo que os decía!
¡ qué pronto en vuestro pecho el ruido anciano!
¡ qué viejo vuestro 2 en el cuaderno!

10   ¡ Niños del mundo, está
la madre España con su vientre a cuestas;
está nuestra maestra con sus férulas,
está madre y maestra,
cruz y madera, porque os dio la altura,
15   vértigo y división y suma, niños;
está con ella, padres procesales!

Si cae — digo, es un decir — si cae
España, de la tierra para abajo,
niños, ¡ cómo vais a cesar de crecer!
20   ¡ cómo va a castigar el año al mes!
¡ cómo van a quedarse en diez los dientes,
en palote el diptongo, la medalla en llanto!
¡ Cómo va el corderillo a continuar
atado por la pata al gran tintero!
25   ¡ Cómo vais a bajar las gradas del alfabeto
hasta la letra en que nació la pena!

Niños,
hijos de los guerreros, entretanto,
bajad la voz, que España está ahora mismo repartiendo
30   la energía entre el reino animal,
las florecillas, los cometas y los hombres.

¡ Bajad la voz, que está
con su rigor, que es grande, sin saber
qué hacer, y está en su mano
la calavera hablando y habla y habla,   35
la calavera, aquélla de la trenza,
la calavera, aquélla de la vida!

   ¡ Bajad la voz, os digo;
bajad la voz, el canto de las sílabas, el llanto
de la materia y el rumor menor de las pirámides, y aun   40
el de las sienes que andan con dos piedras!
¡ Bajad el aliento, y si
el antebrazo baja,
si las férulas suenan, si es la noche,
si el cielo cabe en dos limbos terrestres,   45
si hay ruido en el sonido de las puertas,
si tardo,
si no veis a nadie, si os asustan
los lápices sin punta, si la madre
España cae — digo, es un decir —   50
salid, niños del mundo: id a buscarla! . . .

NOTES

It is to be remembered that Vallejo is not a Spaniard but a Peruvian and that Peruvian Spanish has a flavour all of its own. Most Americanisms and Peruvianisms are explained in the notes corresponding to the poems in which they occur. Only the following occur more than once: *aguaitar*, to wait, keep watch, peer; *pararse*, to stand up. *No más* is used to reinforce another expression and has a sense similar to the English *just*: *aquí no más*, just here. The imperfect subjunctive in *-ara* often has the value of a preterite: *sonara = sonó*.

The following abbreviations have been used: Am., Americanism; Per., Peruvianism; arch., archaism; neol., neologism; coll., colloquialism.

LOS HERALDOS NEGROS

Most of the poems included in this anthology were written in Trujillo in the years 1915–17. *Los heraldos negros* probably dates from March 1917, and *Setiembre* from the last months of the same year. *Dios* was composed in December 1917 on board the ship carrying the poet from Trujillo to Lima. *Ágape* and *La de a mil* were written in Lima in January 1918 and *Heces* and *Los dados eternos* in the following months. Many of the poems were revised.

Los heraldos negros (p. 87)
  4. *empozarse* (Per.), to become dammed up.

Ágape (p. 89)
  The title comes from the Greek word meaning brotherly love and refers to the love feast of the early Christians. See Corinthians xi. 17–34.

La de a mil (p. 89)
  The title refers to the cry of the lottery-ticket vendors. 1000 *soles* was the big prize of the period.
  4. *yanó*: the exclamation " ¡Ya no! " has been converted into a noun. It is similar to the English "Not again!" and expresses an inability to endure any more.
  7. *tantálicos* (neol.), tantalizing.

Absoluta (p. 91)
  The first stanza evokes a winter scene. It is to be remembered that in Peru July and August are winter months. The "hand of water" refers to the winter rains.

Los dados eternos (p. 93)

5. This seems to be a reference to María Rosa Sandoval, of whom Vallejo had been enamoured and who died on 10 February 1918, at the age of 24.

Los anillos fatigados (p. 94)

3. *istmarse* (neol.), to join, meet.

Los pasos lejanos (p. 95)

8. This refers to the picture of the flight to Egypt on the wall.

Enereida (p. 97)

The title is a neologism combining *enero* and *Eneida*. This is a January poem, a poem of the New Year. It is to be remembered that in Peru January is a summer month. The bucolic tone and the theme of renewal and rebirth recall Virgil's *Aeneid*.

2. *pajarino* (neol.), bird-like. It conveys a sense of expansiveness and liberation.

13–14. Vallejo's father was for a time governor of the district of Santiago. The stick is the governor's symbol of authority.

34–35. Santiago Crebilleros Paredes, the blind bell-ringer of the church in Santiago, was extremely popular with the children, whom he used to amuse by telling them stories.

Espergesia (p. 98)

The title is an archaic legal term signifying the passing of a sentence. The poet explains his misery by the fact that fate sentenced him to be born on a day when God was not up to the task of creation.

TRILCE

Most of the poems were written in 1919. *LX* and *LXV* were written in 1918; *XXVIII* in the early months of 1920; *XIX* and *XXII* in August–September 1920 when the poet was in hiding; *XVIII*, *LVIII* and *LXI* in prison (November 1920–February 1921); *XXXVI* in Lima in 1921. Many of the poems were revised and corrected.

III (p. 101)

3. See *Enereida*, ll. 34–35.

6. These are the elder brother and sisters of the poet.

9. *penas* (Am.), the souls of the dead not at rest.

V (p. 102)

1. *dicotiledón*: a composite word explained in l. 5. A cotyledon is the undeveloped primary leaf of a plant. The lovers are two cotyledons blossoming in love.

4. *avaloriados* (neol.), given value.

10. *glisar* (Gallicism), to slip, slide.

17. *grupo bicardiaco*, a group of two hearts.

VI (p. 102)

Though this poem refers to Otilia, it is probable that in the poet's mind she has become confused with other women. One is reminded of the figure of Rita in *Idilio muerto* in *Los heraldos negros*.

3. *otilinas* (neol.), pertaining to Otilia.

19. *capulí*, a typical fruit of the *sierra*, the bitter-sweet capulin berry. Here it is used as an adjective with the sense of *blooming*.

XV (p. 103)

3. *cuja* (Per.), bed.

XVIII (p. 104)

2. *albicante* (neol.), dazzling white. It is created from *alba* and possibly *cal*.

17. *bromurados* (neol.), from *bromuro* (bromide). It seems to imply that the poet is under sedation and is seeing the slopes in his mind as he dozes.

XIX (p. 105)

1. *Hélpide*, a Greek word meaning *hope*.

1. *escampar* (Am.), to take shelter from the rain.

7. *la maría ecuménica*, the soul of mankind which will give birth to a redeemer —love—as Mary gave birth to Jesus.

XXI (p. 105)

1. *arteriado* (neol.) is the equivalent of *veteado*, veined.

14. *ternuroso* (neol.) = *ternura* + *amoroso*.

XXII (p. 106)

4. *Don Juan Jacobo*, Jean-Jacques Rousseau. The poet's ideals are those of the French philosopher.

4. *hacerio* would seem to be a popular or archaic form of *zaherio* (mortification, censure) in the same way as the verb *zaherir* has evolved from the archaic verb *hacerir*.

11. *chirapar* (Per.), to rain and shine simultaneously. A *chirapa* is a sunshower.

16. *éstas colmadas* = *cuando éstas estén colmadas*.

19. *posillos* = *pocillos*.

XXIII (p. 107)

1. *tahona* (arch.), bakery.

1. *estuoso* (arch.), warm.

3. *gorgas*, food given to falcons. By extension the word becomes an image of the children: they are like birds stretching out their necks for food.

9. *estiba*, stowage, reinforces *repartías*.

14–15. ". . . in what toothless gum, in what minute shoot of a tooth . . ."

XXVIII (p. 108)

4. *choclos* (Per.), corn on the cob.

14. *tordillo*, dappled.

16. *tiroriro* (coll.), the sound of wind instruments.

17. *¡Así, qué gracia!*, What's so great about that?

24. *deglusión* = *deglución*.

XXXV (p. 110)

3–4. The programmes of the Lima race-track of the period were colourful and extremely long.

9. *doneo* (arch.), coquettishness, flirting.

11. *de a centavito*, cheap, easy.

11. *por quítame allá esa paja* (coll.) = *por cualquier cosa*. She blushes easily at the slightest thing.

12–13. *celar*, to oversee. She tends to her guest's needs, leaning over the table to serve him his beer, and as she does so her breasts protrude. But the beer her nipples watch over is also that contained in her breasts: her breasts are intoxicating even though they are *sin lúpulo*, have no alcoholic content.

16–18. *núbil campaña*, the campaign waged by Otilia to lure the poet into marriage. She carries it out to perfection with her own inbuilt artillery that has been operating all morning. *Germinales* implies that her weapons are part of her biological make-up.

22. Her fingers, like the pancreatic juices, aid digestion: she prepares a meal easy to digest.

24. *soltar el mirlo* (coll.), to loosen one's tongue.

XXXVI (p. 111)

2. *a las ganadas*, striving to outdo each other.

3. *Amoniácase* (neol.), awakens, comes to life. Ammonia is used to revive those who have fainted.

5. *probables senos*, the potential non-material food of love.

6. *cuanto no florece*, non-existence, a state free of the imperfections of ordinary existence.

11. *todavíiza* (neol.), prolongs, perpetuates.

14. *encodarse* (neol.), to grow an elbow. The verb seems to have been formed from a crossing of *codo* and *encobar* and therefore also includes the idea of hatching.

15. *gago* (arch.), stammering, stuttering. The cobblestones stammer like young children.

16. *ortivo*, emerging from behind the horizon. It is normally used of the rising sun.

16. *aunes* (neol.), potentialities, that which has not yet come into being.

31. *azarea* (Am.), irritates, angers.

XXXVIII (p. 112)

7. *melarse* (neol.) = *hacerse miel, volverse meloso*.

XLV (p. 113)

9–10. *a la caza . . . resaca* is the equivalent of an adverbial clause of time: "as the surf hunts for the keys".

XLVII (p. 114)

1. *ciliado*, ciliated. The poet sees the reef through his eye-lashes as his eyes droop with sleep.

5. *desislarse* (neol.), to cease to be an island, to sink beneath the sea.

12. "laugh like old mice."

18. When Vallejo was a child it was hoped that he might follow an ecclesiastical career.

23. *la 1*, the first hour of existence.

LI (p. 114)

According to Espejo (*op. cit.*, p. 117) this is a love poem addressed to Otilia in which Vallejo adopts the language of a child in an attempt to excuse the harshness with which he treated her.

13. *los* refers to *engaños*.

LVI (p. 116)

4–7. He can never be sure whether such satisfaction as he derives from life is authentic or not. He suspects that it is a form of self-deception, a projection of his own longings on to reality, and that when he comes down to earth all he can do is lament that this, like everything else, has no importance or significance.

LVIII (p. 116)

3–4. There is a play on words: the naked are like clothes which have been crumpled, creased and reduced to rags. *Haraparse* is a neologism.

10. *erogar*, to distribute. It is a legal term.

LX (p. 118)

2. *vejetal* = *vegetal*. This version brings in the idea of *vejez*, of weariness and old age.

4–6. The twelve hours of the clock face are like legs rushing the day towards its end, so quickly that the leagues it covers seem to be rushing in the opposite direction.

17. *sutura*, suture. Men are joined in pleasure.

LXI (p. 119)

18. *se me hizo tarde*, I've been delayed.

27. *puso*: *nadie* is the subject of the verb.

LXV (p. 120)

9. *ayo*, tutor, has connotations of old age: the chair is like an old man entrusted with the task of disciplining and educating a young boy. *ayo* may also have the sense of the French *aieul*: grandfather, ancestor. The chair probably belonged to the poet's grandfather.

10. *quijarudo*, big-jawed.

11–12. "which just stands there remonstrating with my great-great-grand-childish buttocks as tough old leather to tender young leather." The chair is like an old man giving a young boy a dressing-down in a "man to man" discussion.

14. *Estoy ejeando*, I'm striving to get to the essence of myself. The verb is a neologism formed from *eje*. It is reinforced by the image of the sounding-lead.

15. *tascar*, to champ at the bit, to be restless. The trumpets are straining to announce the dawn of a new day, the emergence of what is essential in the poet.

18–20. *los tácitos volantes* are the wheels which operate the human machine, our impulses and emotions. The poet wishes that the wheels might be so set that they function in the same way in all places and in all circumstances, that we might be so purified that, instead of loving only those closest to us and those with whom we have something in common, we embrace all that is distant and foreign to us in a universal love.

25. *humildóse* (arch.), humbled himself, in the sense that he made reverence to his wife's love. The poet's father entered his mother and engendered children in her, but in love he himself was a child seeking a mother's care and protection.

LXXI (p. 121)

11. *polos en guardia*, like extremes defending themselves.

15. *gallos ajisecos*, a class of fighting-cock characterized by its red plumage. *Ají seco,* dried chili pepper, is deep red in colour. The adjective may also have connotations of fieriness.

16. *ennavajados*, armed with razors. This is a technical term employed in cock-fighting. Cocks often have razors attached to their spurs to increase their effectiveness. Here it can be taken as having the sense of doubly armed.

15–17. The lovers are like two fighting-cocks armed with their physical attractions, the curves of their bodies (*cúpulas*), which are incomplete (*viudas mitades*) and need each other to become whole.

LXXVI (p. 122)

6. *chapa* (Am.), lock. He was a lock and key that did not go together; it was impossible to penetrate into his inner world.

LXXVII (p. 122)

6–9. The only conditions in which he can accept to stop living life to the full are if he has to undergo martyrdom in defence of his integrity as a poet, in defence of his right to live life to the full, or if he dies completely saturated, having experienced all the passions and sensations that life has to offer.

POEMAS HUMANOS

In the first edition many of the poems bore dates, but these correspond to the date on which the poems were revised, not to the date of composition. It is therefore impossible to give an exact chronology of all the poems. *Nómina de huesos, Existe un mutilado* . . . and *Voy a hablar de la esperanza* are from the period 1923–8 and should have formed part of *Poemas en prosa. Salutación angélica* and *Altura y pelos* were written around 1932, though a first version of the latter goes back to 1927. *Va corriendo, andando* . . ., *Epístola a los transeúntes, Los nueve monstruos, Considerando en frío* . . ., *Me viene, hay días* . . . and *Parado en una piedra* . . . date from the period 1933–5. *Piedra negra sobre una piedra blanca, Palmas y guitarra, Acaba de pasar* . . . and *¡ Y si después de tantas palabras* . . . *!* were composed around 1936. *Quiere y no quiere . . ., Al fin, un monte . . .,* and *El acento me pende . . .* are from September 1937; *Traspié entre dos estrellas* and *Marcha nupcial* from October; *Un hombre pasa . . ., Hoy le ha entrado una astilla . . ., El alma que sufrió de ser su cuerpo, Al revés de las aves . . ., Los desgraciados* and *Ello es que . . .* from November. *Ello es que . . .* was the last poem written by Vallejo.

Many of the poems did not bear titles. For reasons of convenience I have arbitrarily given such poems a title based on the first line. In such cases the title is followed by three dots.

Va corriendo, andando . . . (p. 125)

5. The preposition *para* and the adverb *entonces* are used as nouns. The function of *para* is to indicate destination and it therefore seems to represent the future that lies in store for man, while *entonces* stands for the past, though it could possibly have a future sense. Man carries his future and past about with him, his condition never changes.

20–21. The confusion of attributes in these lines seems to translate the absurdity of existence: in an absurd world all things become equal in their meaninglessness and tend to be confused. The sense would seem to be that if man covers up the dead leaves, he cannot prevent the tree from dying, and if he coats iron with gold, it still continues to be iron: however much man may close his eyes, he cannot escape or change the reality of things.

Un pilar soportando consuelos . . . (p. 125)

3. *pilaroso* (neol.), pillarish. By creating an adjective from the noun, Vallejo extracts the word's emotive content and puts it into relief.

6. *con asas*, grasping the handles of the cup with both hands.

12. *doses*, duplicates. The numeral is used as a noun.

13–14. These lines seem to be an elaboration of the Peruvian expression *hablar en plata*, to speak with determination and authority. The sense is: "I affirm it with the certainty that it's true."

15. *terceras nupcias*, the marriage to death. The number three symbolizes unity and completeness that is to be found only in death.

17. *vidriera* (Am.), shop window. Happiness is beyond man's reach, behind a window where he can see it but never touch it.

20. *corazónmente* (neol.), heartily. The poet is united body and soul to his skeleton, he has yielded himself up to death.

Epístola a los transeúntes (p. 126)

9. *compañones* (coll.), testicles; (arch.) companions. There is a play on the two senses of the word: his testicles are his companions.

22. *mi cosa cosa*, my sexual organ.

Quiere y no quiere . . . (p. 127)

13. *bimano*, bimane, two-handed. Man is a duality.

19. *cejón* (coll. Am.) = *que tiene mucha ceja*. Here it has the metaphorical sense of frowning.

22. This line is the equivalent of *a ciencia cierta*.

27. *con toda la bragueta*, with virile vigour.

Salutación angélica (p. 128)

6–7. Because of the qualities of these men of various nationalities, it is as if a breath of heaven had reached earth, it is as if the infinite had kissed man on the shoulders. This elaborate poetic gallantry is intended to exalt these men so that the poet can go on to exalt the Bolshevist even more.

14. His complexion is communicating: his sentiments show on his face.

26. *añadido*, extra. When he looks at his fellow men he puts something extra, something that others do not put—his love.

32. The poet accuses himself of vanity, of wanting to be the centre of attraction, of behaving so that others might comment on his acts.

La rueda del hambriento (p. 130)

4. *vacar*, to vacate a post, to be out of a job.

4. *yeyuno*, jejunum, the part of the small intestine between the duodenum and the ileum.

10. *la madre del cordero* (coll.), the cause or origin of something.

15. *calcárida* (neol.) = *calcárea* + *árida*.

Ello es que . . . (p. 132)

4. The map of Spain, which was undergoing the horrors of civil war and being crushed by the forces of reaction, is the symbol of the poet's solidarity with the rest of suffering humanity.

43. The sun casts the rays of the moon: the poet lives in an absurd, chaotic world.

Intensidad y altura (p. 133)

6. *encebollarse* (neol.), to make a stew of oneself. The verb brings in associations of the kitchen as well as expressing the idea of getting bogged down.

7. *voz*: the original gives *toz* which may be a neologism or a misprint for either *voz* or *tos*.

Hasta el día en que vuelva . . . (p. 134)

2. Here Vallejo describes himself in terms of a minute part of his body to insist on his insignificance. His definitive self is born of death: death "defines" man since all his life must be lived in relation to his death.

7. *periplo* (arch.), voyage of circumnavigation.

Los nueve monstruos (p. 134)

25. *la res de Rousseau*, Rousseau's republic. *Res* is probably an abbreviated form of the Latin *res publica*. Rousseau's ideals are the symbol of human progress outstripped by evil.

33–38. Vallejo enumerates the natural misfortunes that befall man and his responses to them. The reiteration of the number nine seems to clarify the title: the nine monsters are the spirit of evil, malevolent spirits spreading suffering in the world.

43. *nos desclava*, suffering un-nails us in the sense that it extracts us from rest, allowing us no repose.

46–51. Vallejo exploits all the possible variants of a formula to enumerate the different effects that suffering has on men. Some are born to the reality of life, they become aware of its absurdity. Others grow in moral stature by the dignity with which they face up to suffering. Others die, are morally crushed by their suffering. Others are born to the reality of life, but without letting themselves be overwhelmed by the absurd. Others are laid prostrate by suffering without ever realizing the absurdity of existence. The majority live and suffer superficially, mechanically, unconsciously, without ever opening their eyes to the absurd and without their suffering affecting them deeply.

60. *un ecce-homo*, a Christ, a victim.

61. *ardio = ardido.*

Sermón sobre la muerte (p. 137)

2–3. *corchete*, bracket, parenthesis, seems to represent man's isolated moments of happiness and optimism; *párrafo y llave* symbolize his writings and ideals of transcendence—in *Poemas humanos* the key opening the door to another plane of reality is frequently used as a symbol of the transcendental; *mano grande y diéresis* convey the idea of gesticulation and emphasis and refer to man's oratory and rhetoric. Death sweeps all these things before it.

6. *este esdrújulo retiro*, the poetry which he cultivates in retreat from the vanities of the world.

8. *en prototipo del alarde fálico*, death is foreshadowed in the sexual act: love is a kind of annihilation in which man surrenders his separate identity; the vagina is the image of the tomb.

25. *caballísimo de mí*: Vallejo creates an adjective from the noun to insist on his animal nature.

30. *brazudo* (coll. Per.), strong-armed.

Considerando en frío . . . (p. 139)

10. *el diagrama del tiempo*: Vallejo tends to see time as a curve sloping towards death.

11. *diorama*: time is like a diorama in that it puts human achievements in a different perspective.

25. *encontradas piezas*, discordant parts. The human body is a machine that functions imperfectly.

Traspié entre dos estrellas (p. 140)

The title seems to express the idea of a cosmic Fall: man has fallen from a happy celestial state to a miserable earthly one. In the poem man appears as a fallen creature. This, of course, is not to be interpreted in a religious sense.

15. *las orejas sánchez = las orejas de Sánchez.* The Sánchez are the ordinary people of the world with ears and noses and no outstanding characteristics.

Hoy le ha entrado una astilla . . . (p. 142)

4. *su centavo*, her poverty. Vallejo frequently employs a small quantity of something to symbolize a lack of it.

Piedra negra sobre una piedra blanca (p. 143)

The title points to the relationship between depression and death. It was suggested to Vallejo during a stroll when, in a mood of black depression and wearing a black coat, he sat down on a white stone. The stone reminded him of a tombstone.

5. *Jueves*, see *Trilce XXXVI*. Vallejo seems to have had a superstition about Thursdays as a day of ill-omen.

7. *a la mala = de mala gana.*

Al revés de las aves . . . (p. 143)

6–9. Suffering and evil have been abolished: there is no more wood or iron than there are left-handed handshakes and consequently the capacity of the cross and the nail for inflicting pain has been reduced to almost nothing.

39. *tartufo*, hypocrite. The word derives from the character in Molière's *Tartuffe*.

El alma que sufrió de ser su cuerpo (p. 145)

1. *glándula endocrínica*, a sickly endocrine gland. *Endocrínica* is a neologism combining *endocrina* and *clínica*.

3. *mi sagacidad* indicates that the poet is adopting the role of the intelligence which makes man suffer by revealing to him the reality of his condition.

7. *tus juanes corporales*, your extremities. The parts of the body assume such importance that they acquire an identity.

30–32. All men, whoever they are and wherever they may be, are in the same situation. In l. 31 the conjunction *o* establishes an equivalence rather than an alternative: man's other self is his abortion and it is also the poet. He is an abortion in that his body is incomplete and imperfect, ugly and repugnant. This line makes it clear that Vallejo is speaking not only with man but also with himself: he insists that his situation is that of all men.

Un hombre pasa . . . (p. 146)

8. *André Breton*, French poet, founder and theorist of the surrealist movement.

Palmas y guitarra (p. 148)

4. *nuestra muerte*: the sexual act is the image of death since the lovers surrender their individual personalities.

6. *tenebloso* (neol.) = *tenebroso + tembloso.*

Me viene, hay días . . . (p. 149)

33. *en su Dante, en su Chaplin*, in his inferno, in his misery. Dante and Chaplin become symbols of states associated with their names.

36. *lleno de pecho el corazón*, my heart is full of love.

Los desgraciados (p. 150)

3–4. "stand up in your head to walk upright", "regain a sense of your own dignity".

5. *saco* (Am.), jacket.

10. *diente* is a symbol of hunger.

15. *fuma*, smoke to deceive your hunger.

16. Instead of having his suffering constantly before his eyes, he should look at his portrait, at himself: he should keep in mind that he is a man and behave with dignity.

20. When he opens his eyes he reawakens to his misery, he takes consciousness of himself and his situation. In this sense it is as if a mirror had been placed before him. Since his eye opens to a world of horror it is as if it had been lashed.

25. *doses*, fellow unfortunates. The number is used as a noun.

27–28. Instead of greeting the new day the *desgraciado* remains silent, discouraged and apprehensive. It is the poet who speaks the words that the *desgraciado's* mouth does not utter.

42–43. The metals are imprisoned in the axe and the axe will be placed at the service of man: the destructive forces of life will be dominated and made constructive.

Parado en una piedra . . . (p. 152)

In *Rusia en 1931* Vallejo says: "Pienso en los desocupados. Pienso en los cuarenta millones de hambrientos que el capitalismo ha arrojado de sus fábricas y de sus campos. ¡ Quince millones de obreros parados y sus familias ! ¿ Qué va a ser de este ejército de pobres, sin precedente en la historia ?" (184).

6. *peciolo*, petiole, leaf-stalk.

¿ Qué me da . . . ? (p. 154)

3–4. The poet confuses objects as distinct as an egg and a coat. In an absurd world all things become equal in their meaninglessness.

Oye a tu masa . . . (p. 155)

1. *cometa*, like other images of flight, of the striving to reach the heights, symbolizes man's spiritual aspirations.

¡ Y si después de tantas palabras . . . ! (p. 155)

10. *tiniebla* and *sombra* are both images of the darkness of death. Life is a death in that it is empty and meaningless and is never fully assumed. In this sense death puts an end not to life but to death.

Nómina de huesos (p. 157)

The title recalls the vision of the prophet Ezekiel (xxxvii. 1–12) of a field littered with bones. For Vallejo the world is a spiritual wilderness and the poem lists the bones that litter that wilderness, the different aspects of man's spiritual death.

Existe un mutilado . . . (p. 157)

6. *Les gueules cassées*, "the smashed faces", an organization of French war-wounded.

ESPAÑA, APARTA DE MÍ ESTE CÁLIZ

The poems were written in the period September–November 1937. A first version of *Masa* goes back to 1929.

Himno a los voluntarios de la República (p. 161)

10. *el vaso de la sangre*, the veins. This indicates how humble his gesture is.

18. *cuadrumano*, quadrumanous, of the obsolete order *Quadrumana*, the Primates other than man.

23. *bienio* refers to the years 1934–6.

24. *morderse los codos* (Per.), to be at the end of one's tether.

26. *tascar frenos*, to champ at the bit.

29. *natalicio* (Am.), birthright, the condition into which one is born.

37. *agujas atmosféricas*, the needles of the compass. Because of the sacrifice of the *miliciano* the winds change direction and death changes key.

40–55. This is a parenthesis in which Vallejo relates the Civil War to the Spanish tradition and explains its significance. This war is *cosas de españoles* but not in the scornful sense that the world uses the term. It corresponds to something eternal in the Spanish soul and there is a continuity linking the great figures of Spanish culture with the heroes of the Republic. Both incarnate the Spaniard's striving to conquer the temporal and achieve the eternal. The difference lies that in the past they sought to transcend the earth and attain heaven: now they seek to conquer heaven on earth. Thus Lina Odena, the popular heroine, is at odds with Santa Teresa, but is also a mystic in her own way.

41. *a quema ropa* (Per.), rapidly. The sense of the line is: "in a quick evaluation".

46. Antonio Coll was a hero of the Civil War. He attacked seven Nationalist tanks single-handed. He is a paladin defending liberty. He serenely steps towards death with a momentary sweat of fear.

49. Santiago Ramón y Cajal was a celebrated Spanish histologist. The *pequeño infinito* is the microscopic world of the histologist who discovers the macrocosm in the microcosm.

57. *una piedra inmóvil*, death. In Vallejo's poetry the stone is frequently a symbol of death.

64. *tu vorágine impelente*, the abyss of death towards which he is lured in order to create a harmonious world.

65. His violence is methodical in that it is based on the theory and practice of collective action.

68. But for the *miliciano* the infinite (*la extensión*) would be inaccessible (*sin asas*).

88. "fabulous beggars of the wealth and well-being that you have produced with your blood."

117–18. The worker lying on his back, in profile, has died to redeem man. In this sense he is not really dead since he lives on in what he has left behind him. Hence the substantivized adverbs expressing the permanence of death are qualified by adjectives expressing impermanence.

120. This is a humorous allusion to the Italian invasion of Abyssinia which preceded the Spanish Civil War.

126–8. The *miliciano*, the child of the earth, is armed only with dust and poverty, but the earth has shod him with magnets so that his march becomes irresistible.

159–61. "I sense this peace when my mind is at rest, and even more so when I am at work, making my voice heard to encourage others."

164. *el genio descalzo*, Christ.